1st edi '93   £4.00

D0835653

The Armchair Sailor

The Armchair Sailor

Bob Fisher

Waterline

For Edward Robert Archer
the first of a new generation of sailors

Published by Waterline Books
an imprint of Airlife Publishing Ltd
101 Longden Rd, Shrewsbury, England

© Bob Fisher 1993

ISBN 1 85310 426 4

A Sheerstrake production.

A CIP catalogue record of this book
is available from the British Library.

The publishers have made every endeavour to trace
the copyright holders and secure permission to
reproduce the extracts included in this work.
Since many of the books are no longer in print and
were published some time ago, this has not proved
possible in every case.

Printed by Livesey Ltd., Shrewsbury, England.

Contents

Preface

During the original planning of this book, I was reminded that there was no yachting joke. At least, that is what my friend and colleague Malcolm McKeag informed a television script writer, adding that the humour in sailing was that it was a series of disasters about which we laughed.

There are some of those within these pages, as no one knows the truth of that more than the writer, who has to be reminded that he doesn't have to requalify for membership of the South West Shingles Yacht Club every year – that august body being open only to those who have committed a serious malpractice afloat and are prepared to tell all afterwards.

The membership includes those who have sunk everything from an outboard runabout to a submarine, and those whose inadvertent actions have made them the temporary laughing stock of the waterfronts. They, more than most, will truly appreciate the fact that there is no yachting joke.

There are, however, many poignant and humorous moments of sailing; a few of which I have tried to tell and others for which I have relied on extracts from the writings of others. This book is a pot-pourri aimed to amuse. It also tries to point to some of the changes that have occurred ever since sailing became a sport and of those which led to its demise as a means of commercial transportation. It does not try to be complete, but merely to scratch the surface, titillate the palate and stimulate those who wish to leave their fireside and join the ranks of those who do, or in some way satisfy those who prefer to watch from the comfort of an armchair in the yacht club window.

Should it have a message, it would be to have fun on the water.

BOB FISHER, *Lymington, May 1993*

Chapter One

Know How

Sailors are oft accused by outsiders of complicating the issue in their use of strange language, nomenclature and jargon. The reverse is really the truth. A sailing boat is a complex unit and for communication purposes it is essential that each part of it is distinctively named, otherwise confusion can arise and that can lead to a chain reaction which, in turn, can lead to disaster. Consider, therefore, what it was like aboard merchant ships prior to the parliamentary act which altered steering orders on board ships flying the Red Ensign.

The New Helm Orders

Up to 1st January 1933 the order 'Port your helm,' or simply 'Port', whether the vessel was being steered by a wheel or a tiller, meant that the vessel should be turned to Starboard. The reason was that originally all vessels were steered with 'tillers', and the order meant put the 'tiller' over to Port, which naturally turned the vessel to Starboard.

No change was made with the advent of the steering wheel until 1st January 1933. Before that date, on the order of 'Port' being given, it meant that the wheel was to be put to Starboard, the rudder went to Starboard, and the vessel went to Starboard (and vice versa for the order 'Starboard').

The Merchant Shipping Act 1932 altered this, and now the order 'Port' means that, whatever the method of steering, the vessel is to be made to turn to Port, and the order 'Starboard' means that it is to be turned to Starboard.**"**

From 'Jottings for the Young Sailor' *by L.F.Callingham*

That book was published for the *Arethusa* Training Ship and the frontispiece shows the *Arethusa* of 1933, a steel four-masted barque, afloat on the River Medway. That same fine sailing ship, under her original name, *Peking*, can now be found at the South Street Seaport in New York, almost completely restored and open to the public who can obtain from her some idea of what life on board the great grain racers was really like. No longer is she a training ship but alongside her the fleet of J 24s of the Manhattan Yacht Club gives sailing to the otherwise deprived 'yuppies' of Wall Street.

They might well want to know the difference between magnetic variation and compass deviation and they could find no better place from which to learn than from the pages of the small book published for those who served aboard the *Arethusa* (née *Peking*) in England.

"*Variation*

The angle between a line drawn from a given position to the Magnetic North and another line drawn from the same given position to the True North is the angle of Variation in that locality and is referred to as 'the Variation.'

Variation may be either westerly as in this country and the Atlantic generally or easterly as in the Far East.

The needle of a compass (in the absence of any disturbing factor) may, for navigational purposes, be taken as pointing to the Magnetic Pole.

It is therefore obvious that a vessel at a given point A intending to proceed to another point B situated to the True North of A would not get to B by steering on a North course as shown by an accurate compass needle, for this needle would be pointing to the Magnetic North (over one thousand miles away from the True North).

In plotting courses and bearings allowance must therefore be made for the amount of local Variation.

On a chart of the English Channel the Variation may be given, say, as follows:

Variation 14 degrees 10' W. decreasing about 12 minutes (12') annually.

This annual decrease is due chiefly to the movement of the Magnetic Pole above referred to.

Gyroscopic compasses, not being controlled by the Magnetic Pole, but by the rotation of the earth on its axis, should point to the True North, but may be subject to a small error depending on the Latitude and the direction and speed of the vessel, which affect the relativity of the earth's axis to the rotary axis of the gyroscope.

Deviation

In the same way that Variation is the angle of difference between the direction True North and the direction of a compass needle pointing to the Magnetic North, Deviation is the angle of difference between the direction of a compass needle pointing to the Magnetic North and the direction in which the deflected compass needle of a ship is actually pointing; like Variation, Deviation may be either westerly or easterly.

It is clear that Deviation only occurs when the compass needle does not point accurately to the Magnetic Pole.

In vessels constructed of wood without engines or ironwork, the Deviation will be negligible, but in vessels constructed of metal or wooden vessels with engines, the Deviation can be considerable, and a cargo of metal or metal fittings also has the same effect.

The chief cause of Deviation in ships with metal hulls is the magnetism of the hull, which is produced by the induction of the

11

earth's magnetism while the vessel is being built. The direction of this force depends in some measure on the direction of the vessel's keel while being built.

Deviation can be corrected to a large extent by counteracting the magnetism which causes it. This is done by scientific placing of magnets and metal round the compass.

The angle of Deviation is not constant, but may vary on each Compass Course steered by a vessel.

It is not difficult to apply Deviation in practice if a vessel is provided with a Deviation Card, which shows at a glance the actual course to be steered after allowing the requisite amount of Deviation for each point of the compass.

In yachts with engines two Deviation Cards may be found to be necessary, one when the engine is out of use and the other when the engine is running, as the electric circuit in the engine may have a serious effect on the compass.

Deviation may vary from time to time in the same vessel, and compasses should be adjusted at least each year as well as before setting out on an extended cruise, and wherever possible Deviation should be checked by comparing the Compass Course with the known Magnetic Course.

Deviation may also vary when a vessel lists or heels over, as this causes a change in the magnetic field. **"**

The boys of the *Arethusa* were left in no doubt as to what was what and by what it was called. They were reminded by Mr. Callingham of why the dog watches were so defined. He drew from Smyth's *Sailor's Word Book*, of 1867 in which 'Dog-sleep' referred to the uncomfortable and fitful naps by sailors when all hands are kept up by stress of weather. The two two-hour Dog Watches that derived; from 4 pm to 8 pm each day; were to change the pattern of the two watches on a ship to prevent monotony. A much more suitable system now used on long distance ocean racers is to break the day into two daylight watches of six hours each and have three four hour night watches.

The instructional books of yester-year have a charm of their own. One of those was part of my father's library and almost certainly the first sailing text book I ever read. Published by the longest name in yachting – Imray, Laurie, Norie and Wilson – before Messrs Imray and Laurie had joined the firm, it is entitled, *Amateur Sailing in Open and Half-decked Boats*. Written by Tyrrel E. Biddle and published in 1886, it combines the author's experience with a genuine sense of terror and some humour. Since a certain amount of my early sailing was in small boats and I was constantly reminded by my father that gybing was a dangerous manoeuvre which could lead to my filling the boat, I used to delight in the passage which told of how Mr. Biddle had encountered a minor disaster through a very simple mistake on the part of his sailing companion.

"*Management of open boats under sail***

Some years ago, I was sailing a skiff with a single lug sail in company with a young friend. The breeze was nice and fresh, but squally, and nothing could exceed the delight of my companion as the little boat dashed the spray from her bow and bounded along.

'What a jolly cruise!' said he. 'How easy sailing is compared to rowing.'

We were sailing with the wind on the quarter; I was steering and holding the sheet in one hand. Suddenly a squall struck us heavily; I let go the sheet; but unfortunately, my friend, instead of keeping on the weather side of the boat, allowed himself to slide down to leeward as she heeled over, and a swish of sea coming at the same time, she filled up to the thwarts.

Fortunately, all the ballast on board was contained in four 28lb. sand bags; to throw these overboard was the work of a moment, and then we set to baling vigorously, because every now and then a wave came leaping over the gunwale. As soon as the water was partially out of her, I crawled forward, unshipped the mast, and we took to the sculls, my friend being only too glad of the exertion to keep himself warm, for he was soaked through.

After a bit we ceased pulling and took a nip of spirits; as my chum tossed off his share, he remarked, 'After all, sailing is very well, but rowing is safer,' an observation with which I cordially agreed under the circumstances.

13

The weight of one man in a 12 foot boat (which was the length of the one in question) on the lee side in a squall was no joke, it is a wonder she did not capsize, which I attributed to her being a broad boat for her length, she was 4ft 6inches beam.**"**

I have to admit to doing my fair share of rowing in the early days, once or twice it was necessitated by filling the boat through inadvertent gybes or a careless broach, and I baled a lot as well.

One thing I had to do; maintain my own boat. Had I read Mr. Biddle on the subject of painting boats, I might well have stuck to cricket. I was able to go to Blyth Bros. chandlery on the Waterside and buy my paint and varnish in tins from the proprietor, Walter Wenlock, whose prices drew for him the soubriquet of a Shakespearian character rhyming with his surname; a century ago, it was not that easy or perhaps that was only because the author didn't want it to be. The last chapter of his book is full of fire and brimstone!

"*Paints & Varnishes, Breaming, Patent Compositions, Cleaning Spars, and Other Hints.*

How few there are, either among yachting or boating men, who understand the art of putting on paint properly. Two persons may use the same paint, out of the same pot, on two different surfaces, and one surface will not only look well, but dry well, while the other will be tacky and smudgy. The first consideration in paints, is to see that the different colours are thoroughly well ground, if not, they will look bad; the next is to see that the oil, turpentine, varnish, patent driers, etc are clean and of uniform good quality. Some amateurs, and indeed, professionals also, will always mix a little gold size with their paints; this they say, gives it a gloss, but, although like terebine it assists the drying, or rather, tends to harden the paint, it darkens the colour, and makes a delicate white quite yellow.

The easiest way for an amateur to go to work, if he wishes to save trouble, is to buy the ready-mixed paints, sold in tins at the oil shops. These will be found to be admirably suited to his purpose; but they require the addition of a little varnish and terebine to make them dry quickly.

To those who prefer to mix their paints themselves, my advice is, always buy the colour required, in dry powder, and then you can see whether it is coarsely or finely ground, and can re-grind it, by wrapping the powder up in a piece of linen or long cloth, and rolling it with a common kitchen rolling-pin, or pounding it with a flat-iron. Put the powder into the pot first, then the patent driers, in the proportion of about one to three, next pour in sufficient boiled oil to cover these ingredients fairly; now with a flat piece of wood about an inch broad, knead the whole together until it forms a smooth, pasty mass, taking care that there are no lumps left. If it is intended as merely a ground-work, or as a priming, in which case it should be either red or white lead; it should be thinned with turpentine to the consistence required, and then applied with a moderately hard brush, in order to rub it well in. If, on the contrary, it is meant as a finish coat, instead of turpentine, varnish should be used to bring it to its right consistency; a small quantity say half-gill to a pound of paint, may be used, where time is an object, and the paint is wanted to harden very quickly.

Before applying the paint, the surface intended to be painted should be rubbed smooth with plenty of wet glass-paper and pumice-stone, and then thoroughly washed and dried with chamois leather. This removes all the grease and dirt, besides making an even surface. All crevices, cracks, and nail-holes should be filled up with a mixture of red lead, common putty, and gold size; this hardens in a couple of days, and can then be rubbed down smooth with glass-paper.

In laying on the paint, take care there are no holidays left, *id est*, places not touched by the brush, or, as boat-painters say, 'knock a piece off'. If the brush is a bad one, or loose from age, throw it away and get a good one; the hairs get into the paint, and nothing looks so bad as to see the marks of the hairs of the brush on a painted surface.

To produce the best white paint for delicate work, I never mix any oil with the colour, as it darkens it, and, in fact, turns it a sickly

15

yellow, as already stated, in time. The best way is to get some white enamel varnish and grind up some white zinc paint, not white lead, as the latter gets black in time. If found too stiff, it may be thinned with some spirits of turpentine – a very little French ultramarine, in the proportion, say, to a pound of paint, of a good sized tea-spoonful, will give additional delicacy to the colour; use no driers; mix it thoroughly, and then strain the whole through a piece of cambric.

When the first coat is dry, go over it with whitening, rubbing it over with the hand; then chamois leather it, to rub off the whitening. The surface will now look quite dull, so the next thing is to bring it up again – mix a little more varnish with your paint, and give it another coat, and when thoroughly dry, which will take from seven to eight hours, rub it all down with pumice stone and water, dry it off, and give it a coat of the varnish itself, and when this last brush over is hard, face it up with white French button polish, and rubbed well over with the indispensable chamois leather. The surface will now look like polished ivory, and friends will ask you, as I myself have been asked, 'How on earth do you manage to get such an ivory surface on wood?'

Speaking of varnishes, they vary considerably, some are good for one thing some for another. I have tried a great many, but my experience teaches me only to trust in those made by manufacturers who make a speciality of yacht and boat-work, and who have a different kind of varnish to suit each purpose; thus, spar varnish is for spars only, or, at least, for bright outside wood-work, such as blocks etc. Then there is inside yacht cabin varnish, and outside yacht varnish; this last is capital stuff for keeping its gloss, even in salt water, a rub with the chamois bringing it up like magic.

Besides these, there are several other descriptions. No 1 boat varnish is excellent for bright wood-work, such as teak or mahogany; but for rough work, I prefer No 2, it is not quite so smooth working but it stands knocking about better, and is, of course, cheaper. No 3 boat varnish is good of its kind, but I would not advise its use, except to mix with paints, such as black, browns and reds; for this purpose it answers capitally.

When buying varnish, always, if possible, go direct to the maker. I have often condemned a varnish purchased at a shop, and found out afterwards that it was not made by the firm whose name was on the can, from whence it was served out to customers – there is no other commodity with which certain tradesmen play such tricks with, as varnish; therefore I say, go at once to the manufacturer or some responsible agent, tell him exactly what you want and then you may depend on getting satisfaction out of your work.

In an old boat that has had successive coats of paint or tar, one over the other, it may be necessary, in order to get a clean surface, to bream her – that is, burning the paint or tar off by means of fire. This operation requires a little care and watching, but is by no means so troublesome as some imagine. All that has to be done, is to place the boat upright on the beach, pile a lot of shavings under her bottom, then stop all leaks and fill the boat full of water; set fire to the shavings, and stand by with a bucket of water, in case the wood itself should catch fire. Two or three burnings, followed by a good scraping, will soon bring the bare wood out, and then her bottom can be freshly painted, or coated with some of the patent compositions so much in vogue now. The fishermen use a sort of 'pickle' as they call it – a mixture of arsenic, vinegar, paint and copperas – but I would not advise it for either yacht or boat, it never looks nice, after the first day or two turning a dirty green colour. Next, there is Peacock's, the best for iron or steel boats, but said to be not so good as Jesty's for wood, although it is after all a mere matter of taste, some preferring one, some another; each has its advocates, and myself have used both without finding any appreciable difference.

A very good composition, and one that stands the water very well, is made as follows:

Take 1 lb. red lead, 4 ozs of copper bronze powder – that at quarter the oz will do – 4 ozs of arsenic, 4 ozs of chrome yellow, 4 ozs paris blue, half lb patent driers, 1 pint of boiled oil, and 1 pint of common boat varnish. Mix the whole together, stirring it round and round, until it comes out a rich copper colour. It will be rather too stiff to work, however, so it must have a little more varnish added until it works smoothly and easily. A couple of coats of this on the bottom looks nice, and will last through an ordinary season especially if the boat is not always kept afloat. The same proportions of ingredients will suit any quantity.

A word or two as regards cleaning spars. It is said that the Detergent, as advertised, is the finest thing out – I cannot say, as I have never tried it; but what the writer has tried, is the new American hollow plane, which answers the purposes of a scraper and glass-paper combined. It can be set so as to only take off the bare varnish and dirt, and then a rub down with fine glass-paper, No 0, and the spar looks like new. Scraping is apt to rough the grain up very much and tear the wood, whereas this canny little tool, does the work kindly and evenly, saving a lot of time, labour and loss of temper.

With respect to scrubbing sails; if you are on a sandy beach, the easiest way is to lay them on the sand, and scour them with brushes and salt water; but this, when done too often, helps to wear out the sail very quickly. A better plan, is to lay them on a wharf or dummy barge, or in a field on the grass, and scrub them with soft soap and warm water, then rinse them well in salt water, and let them bleach in the sun till dry. Always choose a hot, sunny day to scrub sails.

I have, in a former chapter, spoken about the caution necessary in handling small craft, such as open and half-decked boats, in squally weather, and I cannot too often impress upon the novice that one half the accidents which occur in these sort of craft, are preventable ones. The best way is, if you are by yourself, and in any doubt as to what to do in the way of shortening, or feel a want of confidence in your own powers of nautical knowledge, is to down sail and out oars, directly you see the squall approaching. If you are not quite a novice, but can tell a hawk from a hand-saw, you may, if it is not a very heavy squall, shake it out, by sailing a very close luff, and just shivering in the wind, but not so as to take the way off the boat. *Always put the helm down* in a squall, even if going with a free sheet; inattention to this had been the direct cause of more than one fatal accident. Again, as to the main sheet, remember that new rope swells when wet, and kinks, so that it is always best to keep a constant watch on it, to see that it is all clear for running at a second's notice.

As already said, the most dangerous squalls are those which come off highlands, or out of the mouths of creeks and rivers. Another point to bear in mind, is, that a long boat is far safer in a surf or short-step waves than a short one. The latter may be turned end over end, while the longer boat cuts through the top of the wave and meets the other wave as a support before the first one can throw her stern up.

In running in an open boat in a strong breeze and rough water, it sometimes happens that although the wind is freshening, those on board dare not take the sail off for fear of being swamped, this is more often the case when the vessel or boat is loaded with ballast, luggage or passengers. The speed is so great that the water cannot run under the boat fast enough so it rises bodily up on each side some inches higher than the gunwale itself. Anyone taking an ordinary tea-spoon and balancing it on the edge of his tea-cup when full of tea, can see at a glance what would happen if the boat stopped or swerved from her course. A river skiff was once caught in this predicament during a heavy thunder squall, before they had time to lower the sail, and she ran about five miles before those on board could do anything else but keep her straight before it. The best thing to be done under the circumstances, is to make all passengers sit down in the bottom of the boat, and steer straight. I have heard old whalers speak of the same phenomenon when being towed by a struck whale, and once witnessed it myself when running in a gale in a deep loaded ship; but never in an open boat, in the case of the ship, it gave me such a turn for I thought we were going bodily down, that I cannot recall it even now without some of that queer feeling returning. Fortunately, the gale suddenly broke, and she gradually slowed down her speed, otherwise, nothing could have saved her.

In conclusion, in whatever situation you are placed in, always try and keep cool and preserve your presence of mind, once lose command of your nerves, the more quickly you get out of the boat and let someone else take charge the better for all concerned, especially those who may be invited passengers of the fair sex. A practised hand if by himself may be able to rectify a mistake, but when he has ladies on board, they are apt to get nervous and impede one's movements."

From 'Amateur Sailing in Open and Half-decked Boats' *by*
Tyrrel E. Biddle

Male chauvinism in yachting was rife even then, but can you imagine the yachtsmen of today hauling their boats up on to a beach and lighting a fire around them! The mind boggles.

There was a sailor I knew who had his boat built close to a beach (so too was *Windward Passage* on Grand Bahama) and a fast boat it proved to be.

Tom Follett was the man Dick Newick and Jim Morris asked to sail their 40 foot proa *Cheers* in the *Observer* Singlehanded Transatlantic Race of 1968. The boat was built in St. Croix in the US Virgin Islands and it caused a great deal of controversy before it was launched.

The Royal Western Yacht Club, which ran the race, refused its entry. Captain Terrance Shaw, the Sailing Secretary of the Royal Western Yacht Club of England, wrote to the Project *Cheers* team on 25 July 1967, 'The Committee are not altogether happy with the design,' adding that they felt that it could easily be caught aback when the skipper was resting below and that it might then easily capsize.

Correspondence between the two bodies continued until on 20 February 1968, Shaw wrote the final 'not suitable' letter. The race was due to start on 1 June and the final date for acceptance of entries was a month earlier than that. There was only one avenue open to the Project *Cheers* team, Follett had to sail the boat to England to 'prove' her seaworthiness.

The organising club was informed and Follett got on with the job. Only a sailor of Tom's calm with an unshakeable belief in his craft would have accepted the challenge but accept it he did, even knowing, as he had proved, that *Cheers* could capsize. Newick had made alterations to make *Cheers* self-righting in case she was ever caught aback again. Tom left St.

Croix on 31 March and arrived at Gosport on 29 April. In doing so, he had not only proved the seaworthiness of *Cheers* but also completed his qualification sail for the OSTAR. There was not a lot the Race Committee could do but accept his entry.

On the way across the Atlantic to Gosport, Tom Follett tried a new (to him) navigational system.

"Didn't have any problem with navigation on the trip. Weather was usually overcast but the sun would appear now and then long enough for me to grab a quick sight. Stars were no good unless it was flat calm. Too much motion on the boat to bring one down to the horizon. The sun was bad enough but I figured an accuracy of about three miles which suited me. Before I left St Croix, Red Stolle told me about a system called 'HO 249' which is a set of sight reduction tables. I had always used my own system which required nothing more than a slide rule or a set of trig. tables but HO 249 looked pretty good and I bought a couple of volumes. One to take me from the equator to 39 degrees and the other from 40 to 60 degrees. I didn't worry about going north of the Arctic Circle.

I've been wasting my time all these years! HO 249 is so simple! Worked out a system where I don't worry about DR at all. A latitude is necessary now and then since one can't be too far away on that but I work backward from HO 249 to figure out an assumed longitude. Apply corrections then and the job is done.

Only time I had difficulty at all was just before entering the English Channel. No sights to amount to anything for about three days. But my transistor radio picked up the Ploneis Consol station and I eased into the Channel on bearings from him plus later bearings from Round Island and Ushant. Hit the Ushant Light (no damage) on course and on time. A little radio like that is quite handy. Takes up very little space and is useful for bearings in bad weather. Not really bang on for accuracy of course but, if one takes this into consideration, there is no difficulty.

While still a good thousand miles out from England I picked up the BBC on 200 kcs. and got some good jazz to listen to as well as shipping forecasts and news. Later on I could pick up the Home service on the broadcast band for a source of nearly continuous entertainment. Can't think why some British don't like the BBC. Best system in the world I reckon. Not that I've heard radio all over the world but I have listened here and there and been pretty much disgusted. The only hope in the USA, for example, is the odd FM station one finds around a few of the large cities. But the British really have something worthwhile in the BBC. The French have a good system too I suppose but they talk too much. I prefer the sound of music to that of the human voice even though the French language is rather pleasant.

Enough about radio, I could carry on like this for a long time. Would you like to hear my views on government?**

From 'Project Cheers' *by Tom Follett, Dick Newick and*
Jim Morris

Nothing would give me greater pleasure than to listen to Tom's views on government. They would be as refreshing as Tom himself was. There was about him, always, a touch of naivety. And there is a great deal of difference between naivety and ignorance. Sometimes the latter may provide unexpected pleasure and sometimes, as Michael Green fictionalised, the lack of knowledge may just allow that enjoyment for a limited time.

**We had a cup of tea and discussed what to do next. Norwich seemed a long way away and the trip would mean a lot of quanting because of heavily wooded banks. Arthur wanted to stop at Brundall so that he could visit the railway station there, which he said was the scene of an historic collision many years ago, but we overruled him and decided on Bramerton Woodsend, a quiet, pretty spot a mile or two beyond Brundall.

It was heavy going. The tide turned against us and we swung the quant pole until our arms ached. It was well after tea-time when we reached Bramerton and we were all so hot and tired that we stripped off for a swim, with the exception of Sheila, and Beaver, who remained unconscious.

That was a delightful swim. I don't think I have ever had a better. We plunged and gambolled around as merry as crickets. Sheila sat in the boat and threw bread to us and we all pretended to be ducks. Then Arthur did his imitation of a submarine, Harry tried to life-save Joan (and nearly drowned her) and Dennis chased a swan.

When the fun was at its height a small child rowed towards us inexpertly and sat staring.

'Hullo, sonny,' I said jovially, catching hold of his gunwale for a rest. 'Aren't you coming in for a swim?'

He didn't reply at once, but continued to brood. He then delivered himself of the following dictum: 'I suppose people have got to go to the lavatory, haven't they?'

I didn't like this.

'Yes', he went on. 'My dad won't let me swim in the river here. It's the sewage, he says.' The sun went in. Somehow the water didn't seem so nice. Arthur was just diving under the surface and spouting like a whale. I shuddered.

The relentless child went on: 'It comes down on the ebb tide from the dyke, my dad says. My dad says he wouldn't swim in this part of the river for all the beer in Norwich, my dad says.'

'Where's the sewer?'

The boy pointed to a bend in the river. 'Just round the corner. They open the gates when the tide's ebbing, like what it is now.'

I did not swim madly to the bank. I kept my head, paddling very carefully in a bizarre fashion, holding my body perfectly upright with my face as far away from contact with the water as possible. I dare not open my mouth, I didn't warn the others until I reached the bank. The effect was rather interesting, like the result of ringing the Lutine Bell at Lloyds.

Joan went berserk, poor girl, and shrieked, 'Oh no, it's all your fault, Dennis,' and swam to the bank as if pursued by a jet-propelled piece of effluent. Dennis went pale and tense and by some remarkable feat of muscular control actually launched himself out of the water from the waist upwards and moved vertically to the bank. Arthur feigned indifference and hooted with

23

bucolic laughter, but I noticed he got to the bank first.

We were only just in time. The sewage dyke announced its presence in no uncertain fashion five minutes later. Looking on the chart we found the following legends marked near our mooring:

Sewage Works (Norwich Corporation) ; Sewage Farm ; Sewage Wharf; Sewage Dyke ; Sewage Outlet ; Old Sewer.

For good measure the bank was marked as lined with old wrecks and there was an inscription: 'Palaeolithic Implements found A.D. 1926.' What a place to put Palaeolithic implements. But as Arthur said, it was just as well we hadn't looked at the chart or it would have spoiled a lovely swim.**"**

From 'The Art of Coarse Sailing' *by Michael Green.*

Like Green's characters, there are yachtsmen who will capitalise on the mistakes they and others make; and, what is more, they will laugh at it, particularly when they can fool others. The inadvertent change of colour in an order for a boat led to the hilarious tale which Olympic bronze medallist, Owen Torrey, was able to tell in *One Design and Offshore Yachtsman*.

"*The Year of the Black Deck*

It all started when the girl in the office at Derecktor's got confused filling out a work order for Bus Mosbacher's new One Ton boat. It was supposed to have black topsides and a white deck and somehow or other things got transposed. Anyhow, the boat came out with white topsides and a black deck. Bus was pretty upset because everybody knows that a boat with a black deck can get pretty hot and uncomfortable in the summertime, but there wasn't time enough before the One Ton Regatta at Newport to do anything about it. The boat was late already. So Bus took it to Newport the way it was and raced the whole Regatta.

It was pretty grim going because the weather was uncommonly hot and the temperature in the cabin hovered around 120 degrees. It wasn't much better on deck either, especially if you tried to sit down.

Being the fine unflappable sailor that he is, Bus nevertheless managed to win the series, which had attracted rather more than the usual coverage by the press. I guess that's what led to some of the trouble because there were a lot of reporters on the dock after the last race trying for interviews. One in particular, a very pretty non-sailor from the *Christian Science Monitor*, was especially insistent. Bus answered her many questions with his usual graciousness but the ordeal of sailing five or six long races in an oven had nevertheless worn him down a little. Inevitably, he was asked what single thing was most responsible for his victory. He replied, just a little brusquely perhaps, that it was obviously the black deck, and in due course it all appeared that way in the press.

A lot of people wondered why a black deck would make a boat go any faster but it wasn't long before a number of them appeared on the race courses around the country. Speculation continued as to the merits of the black deck, and in due course a number of technical articles on the subject appeared in the yachting magazines. One of the most widely read of these was by John Stanton in *Sail* who explained at considerable length that the warm air rising from the deck would inhibit the flow of wind around the underside of the mainsail from the windward side to the leeward side. This was characterised as an 'Induced Collateral End Plate' which served to double the effective aspect ratio of the rig. There must have been some merit in the argument for very soon considerably more black decks appeared on the race courses around the country.

Unfortunately, these were no more comfortable than Mosbacher's had been. Some people even began to wonder whether the extra speed attributed to the black deck was worth the discomfort. Luckily, at this point a number of marine suppliers, especially West Products, came out with some partial remedies for the problem. A new super light insulating material was developed with which to line the overhead. It was sort of unsightly and a little expensive to install but there is no doubt that it helped. On deck the problem was eased by special insulated Topsiders and racing shorts and slacks with special insulation in the seat.

By this time, there were enough black decks in evidence so that the International Technical Committee of the IOR decided to make a study. Pending the results of their investigation, it was decided to assess an arbitrary ¾'s of 1% penalty on the rating of any boat with a black deck. Not to be outdone, the Storm Trysail Club concluded that the ITC's penalty was probably wrong and assessed one of their own which was ⅞'s of 1%. When these penalties were announced, a number of owners who had previously been on the fence concluded that there must indeed be some merit in the black deck, and so quite a few more appeared in the various racing fleets.

Naturally, the matter came to be referred to the various naval architects for opinions. The most complete reply, in terms of words per unit of message, came from S & S who put out a document which might be called a 'White Paper on Black Decks'. It ran on for several very well written pages and concluded with the observation that although any number of colours might be selected for the purpose of painting a deck, black was certainly the darkest, at least so far as that term is commonly understood.

By this time, a number of variations on the theme of 'Basic Black' had appeared. After it was learned that the report that Hard sails had obtained a patent on plain black paint was proven to be untrue, most people followed the obvious course and used it. A few followed more esoteric routes, however. For example, Jessie Phillips had a special mixture prepared for *Charisma*, in which pulverised Titanium was used as the pigment. This was of course a lot more expensive, but it was somewhat lighter and became generally known as 'Light Black'. Doctor Jerome Milgram, former Thistle sailor, stole a march on the fleet by using midnight blue instead of black, thus avoiding the rating penalty. This took the ITC by surprise and they began to investigate the possibilities of using a light meter to measure the reflection of the surface, regardless of colour. Meanwhile, pending the results of this investigation, an arbitrary 10% rating penalty was assessed against Professor Milgram's boat.

Another clever variation was conceived by Britton Chance for Jack Potter's *Equation*. It was found that whatever the merits of a black deck might be in the sunlight, these did not apply at night, and there were, at night at least, some disadvantages. Accordingly, Britt designed a deck which consisted of a series of louvres, somewhat reminiscent of Venetian blind panels running athwartships These were painted black on one side and white on the other and by the simple operation of a hydraulic control, they could be rotated so as to expose either the white side or the black side. This might have proved unreasonably expensive on an ordinary boat, but as *Equation* was already fitted with a very sophisticated hydraulic system for her keel and bomb bay doors, it was a simple matter to include the deck as well. The arrangement worked beautifully and the pumps were easily able to keep up with the leaks.

By the time the next year's Bermuda Race rolled around, virtually the entire fleet was equipped with black decks. Unfortunately, it was a very slow, long and hot race. Even with the specially insulated and air conditioned boats and the special clothing, many of the crews became so exhausted that they were forced to withdraw when the wind died as they neared Bermuda.

Surprisingly enough, the race was won by Bus Moshbacher who unlike his competitors, was as fresh as a daisy when he stepped ashore. It seems that after considerable argument with Derecktor, he had finally succeeded in having the error rectified and his deck painted white. Bus had little to say about his victory except a casual remark to the effect that 'We just kept her moving all the time.**"**

Life and sailing were meant to be like that, tongue in cheek. The sport is, after all, about having fun; or it should be and the more that you know how, the more fun is readily available, if knowing how is a means of avoiding the pitfalls.

27

Chapter Two

The Olden Days

'In olden days a glimpse of stocking was looked at as something shocking,' wrote Irving Berlin. Among the waterfronts, nothing could have been closer to the truth; yachting was a bastion of the male. Women formed a far lesser part of general society at the beginning of the Twentieth Century than they do now and the higher the social stratum, the less they were found with their menfolk. It was an ironically formed society where wives and mistresses met and ignored the fact that they were dependent on the same man; loathed each other; and were often kept apart with the mistresses receiving more of the treats than the wives. *Plus ca change!* For that reason, the women who were to be found around yachting would have had no place in the clubs.

Eventually, however, changes were wrought and women began to appear upon the scene. One of them was Rosa Lewis, the chatelaine of the Cavendish Hotel in Jermyn Street. Rosa took a house in Cowes, one suspects to keep an eye on her clientele, and was very much part of the scene there between the wars. No one recorded the changes that came about better than Anthony Heckstall-Smith, the son of 'Bookstall', in his classic documentary, 'Sacred Cowes'. He knew Rosa well and, her apart, for him, the only ladies of interest were those in some way attached to the Royal Yacht Squadron.

"If the rigs of the yachts underwent a revolutionary change in the twenties, so did women's fashions. Now skirts scarcely reached to the knees, and waists as well as bosoms along with jackyard topsails and bowsprits, disappeared. Under cloche hats that looked like inverted flower-pots, nearly every pretty girl wore her hair bobbed, shingled or cut short in an 'Eton Crop.'

On the day when one of these modern young things tripped on to the Squadron lawn actually wearing trousers – sailor's trousers and a sweater – the outraged members decided that the time had come to call a halt to the progress of fashion. A Committee meeting was held at which it was voted that any lady wearing trousers should be forbidden entry into the R.Y.S. gardens. That momentous decision was taken in the summer of 1924 and, in spite of the changing times, was strictly enforced for the next fourteen years. In 1938 it was relaxed somewhat when ladies were allowed to enter the gardens wearing trousers at any time except during Cowes Week.

But in the twenties, the ladies and what to do with them were problems that began seriously to exercise the distinguished members of the Royal Yacht Squadron. In those days only on the rarest occasions were ladies allowed to cross the threshold of the clubhouse. Escorted by a member, they could view the cups displayed in the club and on the last day of the regatta watch the fireworks from the Platform. At other times they were only permitted to take tea, iced coffee, and eat cakes and strawberries and cream on the lawn to the music of Mr Clifford Essex's band in the afternoons and listen to that same band in the evenings after dinner while the fairy-lights twinkled in the laurel bushes. But at all times they must wear the round cardboard badges, without which they could not pass the ever watchful eye of Wagstaff, the signalman at the gate. Needless to say that those badges were the most coveted emblems and the possession of one marked its wearer's social success at the regatta.

While for more than a century the courteous and chivalrous gentlemen of the Squadron had enjoyed entertaining their ladies upon the lawn, none of them appears to have given a thought to their creature comforts, for, not to put too fine a point on the matter, there was no accommodation of any sort for ladies within the gates. But, so far as one knows, this point entirely escaped the notice of members until that particular afternoon in the summer of 1924 when the first woman set foot on the lawn in trousers for the first time. Then it was argued that if women went sailing in trousers but were not allowed to enter the precincts of the Squadron wearing them, reason and modesty decreed that accommodation must be provided where the forbidden garments could be discreetly removed. Faced with the difficult problem, the members turned their eyes towards Castle Rock, the house across the road where once Mrs Cust had entertained their Commodore and Admiral, King Edward VII. Now, almost miraculously, Castle Rock was put up for sale by the Trustees of the Cust Estate. The property consisted of a small house and garden and a separate ball-room or pavilion. The last was all that remained of Hippisley House an 'elegant Gothic residence' that had once been owned by George III.

If the members of the Squadron could acquire Castle Rock they would not only solve the vexed problem of accommodating their ladies, but protect themselves from anyone undesirable becoming a next door neighbour. So at the Spring meeting, the Committee were instructed to negotiate the purchase of the property, and while the price to be paid was left to their discretion, they were told they could make any reasonable bid in order to buy it.

But to the intense chagrin of the Squadron members they found that they were not the only customers in the market. A mysterious stranger was ready to cap every offer made by the club. For more than a year, the battle for Castle Rock raged, and then in the following August the Committee admitted in their report that they had lost. While there was no chance of buying the house at any figure the club could afford, they said that there was still a possibility that they might be able to buy the ballroom. But even over the latter there were endless delays since the mysterious stranger, who had for so long frustrated them, was now possessed of Castle Rock.

In the Spring of 1925, it was announced that the famous Rosa Lewis – owner of the Cavendish Hotel in Jermyn Street, friend of King Edward VII and Lord Ribblesdale, the 'Ancestor' of Sargent's portrait – was the new owner of Castle Rock.

No one will ever know what prompted Rosa to buy the property. There is no doubt that she paid a high price for it, since she out-bid the R.Y.S., and, once it had become hers, she seemed distinctly pleased with herself and loved to talk of her 'little place' at Cowes. I like to think she bought it out of sentiment, possibly to help the relatives of the late Miss Emma Cust, its late owner, for Rosa was a big-hearted creature. Of course, she could have bought it simply to annoy certain members of the Squadron – contemporaries of King Edward's who may have annoyed her in some way or another – for she never forgot a slight or what she considered a personal injury. But whatever her reason, the remarkable Rosa bought Castle Rock, and, having done so, she condescended to let the ball-room to the Squadron as the Ladies' Annex.

As she so caustically remarked: 'While they won't 'ave me on their old lawn, I'ave to let their lady friends into my garden to piddle.'

Four years later, after much haggling and greatly to her financial advantage, she finally sold the ballroom to the R.Y.S.

In her way, the fabulous Rosa Lewis added considerably to the gaiety of Cowes, for she kept the same open house to the same bizarre assortment of people as she did at the Cavendish Hotel, which the gossips have said was given to her as a present by Edward VII. It was always a matter for speculation who one might meet at Castle Rock when one dropped in of an evening. Younger members of the Royal Family, elderly peers, who had once courted their hostess in the days of her youth, pretty actresses for whom Rosa had promised to find a wealthy husband, young Americans, who she was mothering with extreme indulgence, and always the odd, balding American business man who was never quite sober, but at Rosa's command, generously paid for everyone's drinks.

Sometimes she held impromptu roulette parties when Lord Birkenhead, 'Dick' Charteris, old Henry Denison and others would drop in from the Squadron across the road for a flutter. To Castle Rock all and sundry were welcome, provided they met with Rosa's approval. There was always plenty to eat and an abundance to drink in a carefree atmosphere, for, as Rosa so often said, 'there was no standin on ceremony.' And, indeed there was not, for I once heard her round on Prince George, Duke of Kent who requested a private room that he might entertain his guests.

'A private room?' Rosa said, her voice rising with indignation. 'A *private* room, did you say? Whatever for? If my friends aren't good enough for you to mix with, my boy, you know what you can do.'

After he had taken her hint, Rosa turned to me and said with a chuckle: 'I've know 'im since 'e was in diapers. 'E's a nice boy, but his mother should have smacked 'is bottom more orfen!'

Rosa was certainly no respecter of persons, and I well remember a night when she decided that the roulette party attended by Lord Birkenhead, Henry Denison and some others whose names I have forgotten, must come to an end.

'Now go on 'ome, all of you,' she ordered. 'Pick up your pounds and fivers and be orf!' And with that, she swept the green baize cloth from the tables, scattering the shillings and half-crowns over the carpet.

I recall Henry Denison stooping to retrieve his money.

'No, 'Enry, no,' Rosa chided. 'Now don't be so bloody stingy – leave all that chicken-feed for the poor cleaners in the morning.'

Old Henry Denison was a picturesque survival of the Victorian era, who dressed in a flamboyantly eccentric manner. His clothes always seemed many sizes too large for him, his flowing bow-tie appeared in danger of coming undone, his brightly coloured socks tumbled about his ankles, and the petals of the enormous flowers in his buttonhole were ever about to fall. He was by way of being a ladies' man and an inveterate gossip – a carrier of scandal and a passer-on of tittle-tattle. I remember him best as seated in a basket chair on the lawn, one thin leg wound around the other, thumb thrust in waistcoat, silver-headed cane in hand, piping spiteful witticisms in the ear of some dowager or another. In the evening, while the band played on the lawn, he spent a great deal of his time making sure that no intruder had managed to gain entrance under the cover of darkness. The story goes that once when thus engaged he surprised Princess Beatrice hidden behind some shrubs and guarded by her lady in waiting, coping with an emergency for the relief of which the Ladies' Annex was so belatedly purchased. So shocked was the old gentleman that he departed from Cowes by the first packet steamer the following morning.

I suspect always that Henry Denison was one of the 'Pillars of Society,' and it might well have been he who was once overheard to remark that he always blackballed candidates when the wind was in the east. At one time in order to qualify for membership he must have owned a yacht, but when I remember him he never went to sea and spent his days strolling round Cowes visiting his friends. Rosa was one of his particular cronies, and it was obvious that he had known her in her hey-day, for he still treated her gallantly and one felt that he considered his shuffling visits to Castle Rock to be slightly *risqué* adventures. Of course, around her roulette table he picked up plenty of titbits of gossip with which to entertain his friends the next day.

At the bottom of her garden at Cowes was a little glass-fronted summer-house, where Rosa loved to sit with her special friends watching the passing scene between sips of champagne and commenting on the manners and morals of the passers-by. She was quite remarkably well-informed upon such matters, and thoroughly enjoyed enlightening her guests. It was not surprising therefore, that there were some who feared her scrutiny and hugged the wall immediately beneath the summer-house. But they seldom escaped.

'Look,' Rosa would say, nudging a friend, 'there goes old Lord So-an-So. He thinks I 'avent't seen him. Silly old man! If his wife knew what I know about 'im she'd take an 'airbrush to 'im!'

Undoubtedly, there were some to whom Rosa's presence as the chatelaine of Castle Rock was a distinct embarrassment. But for most of us, she added to the delights of Cowes Regatta. It was a sad day when she finally sold the house and departed, declaring:

'The fun's all over, m'dear. We won't none of us see no more of that sort of thing. The war's put paid to that little lark.'

Of course, by the time Rosa came to play hostess at Castle Rock, she had already been immortalised in the character of 'Lootie Crump' in Evelyn Waugh's *Vile Bodies* and in Shane Leslie's *The Anglo-Catholic*, so that she had become a character and the younger set lionised her as someone worthwhile knowing. Undoubtedly, she had always been a character, and one had only to see the drawing of her by Sargent, that used to hang in the Cavendish Hotel, to realise that she had once also been a beautiful woman. For all her bawdiness, she was a generous and sincere friend. At the height of the blitz and when she was quite old she travelled in her ancient Rolls down deep into the country especially to visit a young wounded sailor and to bring him a hamper of chicken, eggs, butter and champagne.

As often as I think of Rosa, I remember an incident that occurred many years ago at the Cavendish. I had been staying the night in the hotel on my way through London. It was at the height of the Season and the place was full with the usual bizarre collection of guests, and since Rosa had been in one of her expansive moods, we had all sat up half the night drinking champagne in her little sitting-room just off the hall.

The next morning, I was up early to drive down to Southampton, and was astonished to find Rosa waiting to see me off. She was wearing her famous fur coat – the 'sables of sin,' she called it – over her nightdress, and was clutching a bottle of champagne in one hand and a glass in the other.

Suddenly, out of the sunlit Jermyn Street, there appeared a pretty young girl, selling flags.

Rosa looked her up and down with a bloodshot eye. 'What the 'ell do you want at this time in the morning?'

The girl looked frightened, but held her ground. Then, she whinnied nervously, 'Please will you spare something for the blind?'

'The blind! The blind!' Rosa screamed. 'Look 'ere, young lady, I'm blind, the guests are blind, and the staff's blind. And you can bugger orf!'

But before the terrified girl reached the door, Rosa shouted at her to stop.

"Eckstall, give the poor little rotter a sovereign,' she commanded. And as I hesitated to dispense such largesse, Rosa said, 'Come on now. Don't be mean. You've been drinkin' on the 'ouse all night, 'aven't you?'

Rosa is dead and the Cavendish Hotel has been demolished. And, recently, two biographies have been written about her. In my opinion neither of them did justice to her, for they failed to capture her true personality.

As a final tribute to Rosa, I think it should be put on record that it was she who saved the highly distinguished company of ladies who once graced the Squadron lawn a great deal of inconvenience."

From 'Sacred Cowes' *by Anthony Heckstall-Smith*

Rosa Lewis was like W.C.Fields, when it came to children; I was very young when introduced to her, but I quite understood her reaction; she did much, however, to revolutionise Cowes. One would like to think that she approves of what goes on at Castle Rock forty years after she sold it. It may not have quite the same feel as when it was her house but the parties there are none the worse for that. It, or its custodians, still maintains that slightly outre attitude to life of which Rosa would have approved. Within its precincts, ladies have a fairer run perhaps than she would ever have envisaged for anyone but herself, but not, perhaps, the 'complete' equality sought by the feminists that made the eighties so unpleasant for the chauvinist males.

Rosa's attitude would have found favour with Tom Diaper. Even though they were alive and in Cowes during the same era, he was a man she would not have known or recognised, for Rosa was a snob and Tom was one of the lower orders, a professional racing sailor who made it all the way to skipper.

Before he died, Tom Diaper wrote his memoirs on the pages of an old exercise book in a large, sprawling and tremulous hand; the spelling was eccentric and the syntax decidedly irregular but, when it was given to a publisher, he took the refreshing attitude that little should be altered. The result, *Tom Diaper's Log*, is a wonderful insight into the life of a yacht hand of the day.

Tom wrote as he talked, and in this extract his forcefulness and seamanship shine through. He wasn't one to cover his ability in modesty. The chapter from which it is taken is headed thus:

'Now I could pick 35 men . . . and only have one gentleman to take the time and a Yankee to represent America, him to see fair play and myself in command. I would sail *Shamrock IV* and I tell you I would beat the *Resolute*.'

There was no hiding Tom's light under a bushel but he does have a tale to tell of taking one of the *Shamrocks*, the little written about 23-Metre, across the Atlantic for Sir Thomas Lipton, and his subsequent adventures and attitudes.

For 1920 I had shipped in the *Shamrock* twenty-three-metre as second mate under my brother, Alf Diaper, who was the skipper of her. We started on the 15th February to make her ready to cross the Atlantic to act as trial-horse to train and tune up the *Shamrock IV* which was already over there. She went over in 1914, only the war came on. The *Shamrock* twenty-three-metre was not one of the *Shamrocks* built for the *America's* Cup, but built to race around the British coast regattas, so, as I said, we started to make ready.

The *Shamrock* twenty-three-metre was over at Camper and Nicholson's yard. Jim Gilby, the mate was getting her ready with the port watch for the crossing under her ocean rig. She was being made into yawl rig for the crossing, while I, the second mate, with the starboard watch, was cleaning and making and packing all her racing gear – sails, spars, and all the halyards, etc – and labelling it to go across in one of the Cunard boats; we had to take the weight of everything. Quite a big job it is to pack a twenty-three-metre racing gear, but we managed to get it done by the 1st April, and the *Shamrock* was launched and towed out of the river. The compass was adjusted and we moored off Southampton on the Test.

The next day, 2nd April, we went for a short sail with the owner on board. While I was steering her back to her moorings, he wished us luck and hoped I would keep a good log of the voyage across, as, after it was all over, he wanted the log book in London to read to his guest when he came to dinner, which had been arranged whether we won or lost. He hoped there would be something in the book to start a big laugh. So Sir Thomas Lipton and his guest, Lord Delaware, wishing us a good and quick voyage across the Atlantic, with 'God speed you' they went ashore.

The next day, 3rd April, all hands went on shore and signed on to take *Shamrock* twenty-three-metre to America and bring her back to Southampton after the races for the *America's* Cup, whether they won or lost, if required to do so. We left Southampton 5th April and let go anchor off Yarmouth, Isle of Wight, for the night to catch a fair ebb-tide through the Needles passage, for the wind was dead against us all the way down the English Channel.

We left Yarmouth on the morning of the 7th April 1920 and sure enough had the wind ahead the whole way down to Falmouth, where we put in and anchored so that we might do some little alterations what wanted doing for the passage across. It was well for us we had done so, for that night it came on to blow a very hard gale, continuing for almost a fortnight. Then the gale fined down to a light wind.

We left Falmouth and had got about thirty miles to the south-west of Land's End, when the gale came on with redoubled fury. So we ran back to Falmouth again. On the fourth day in there, we made another start, the wind still hanging in the west. We made the first leg of our journey to Ushant, when we put her on the other tack, standing off to make a good clearance of that dangerous point, the wind beginning to increase and the sea getting up. We kept tacking her up to the windward till the third night out of Falmouth, no one getting any rest, it was so rough.

On this third night out I went on watch at 12 o'clock midnight, I had just relieved them when an able seaman asked me to take a look around the forecastle. I did, and quickly got the captain and navigator to look also. This is what I saw. An iron stanchion in the

37

centre of the forecastle, which was a deck support, was starting to bend, which should not have been, but the pounding of her long bow and the heavy seas pounding her deck was causing that – and not only that. The fishplate what ran around each side of the ship, underneath the covering board, was half-inch steel plating and it was bending the port and starboard in line across the deck with the iron stanchion, all in a line bending together.

Myself, having had more than anyone on board of sea-going, in that class of ship, warned that if we kept on pounding her bow in such a storm much longer, the *Shamrock* would not reach America. Why not then turn back and wait for a better chance of luck and a fair wind? The skipper and navigator together said, 'We dare not turn back for Sir Thomas Lipton wants this boat in America.'

I myself answered, 'To h.. with Sir Thomas! He looked out for himself not to be here with us. There are twenty-two of us on board, and sixty-eight in England depending on us. What will they all do if we are lost? The owner cannot look after them, and you know the boats is no good to save us. Now will you listen to me this once, for I have had a lot of experience in this kind of craft. It is 12.20 and I will try to keep her going until 2 am, and if it is no better by then I will turn her round and make for the first port we can reach in safety. The only way you will get this boat to America is by running away from it now in this storm. I will take the blame, if there is any.'

So that was agreed on. They went below, being worn out by their long watch on deck in the gale. The strain had told on the skipper who was ill; it was physically impossible for him to carry on longer on deck. At fifteen minutes before 2 am, I called an able seaman, saying, 'go below, see the first mate, tell him to get all hands out and make ready to turn the ship round.'

So when the first mate came on deck, he said, 'the skipper wants you, the weather is worse now, Tom.' I replied, 'at times it's a devil of a lot worse.' I went below.

The skipper said, 'what is it like on deck, Tom? It is hard enough below.' I said, 'it's that bad, skipper, that I have warned the watch to just rope themselves, for you have a hard job to see the big ones coming. Skipper, it will be risky job turning her in this hurricane.'

'Are you going to wear or gybe her, Tom?'

'No, neither. I am going to stay her' (or, in plain words, tack her round), and I am steering her.'

To the navigator, I said, 'After I get her round, I will see what is on the log and keep her north-east course till I report to you.'

The skipper gave me a tot of whisky; 'I don't want this to buck me, only for good luck,' I said. Then I went on deck, saw the first mate. I said, 'Jim, I will take the wheel, for I am going to sail her until everything is ready for tacking.' 'Yes, Tom,' he answered.

'Now you Jim,' I said, 'go forward to the main rigging. Have a rope to put around you for safety and when I call out to you, you will be looking for a dark spot in the waves. Call out like hell, 'A dark spot Tom.' Then I will, if I have enough way on and the ship answers all right, lee-ho, and every man for himself.'

So only a short space of time had gone by, and I had offered up a short prayer, for guidance and safety in the job I was going to do – the same as I had always done since I started going to sea, to the only One up above Who can see you safely through anything, good or danger, if you ask Him – when the mate's voice came, 'A dark spot coming, Tommy.'

'All right,' I answered, 'and every man for himself.'

Now every man was at his station and everything went just like clockwork. We got that ship round, in spite of the mountainous seas and a hurricane of wind and dark as a dungeon, as well as if we were on a mill-pond, without shipping a pail of water, or breaking a rope yarn.

That was the time that Sir Thomas Lipton ought to have been with us, trying to cross the Atlantic. So having got her round, I set the course north-east, and went below to report to the navigator the course and distance on the log, and had put the oil bags over. Then, turning to the captain I said, 'I don't think a tot of whisky would hurt the men. It will act like medicine. I will enter it in the official log as such'.

39

'Well, Tom' he said, 'I reckon you all deserve it; you all done a good job. I really thought I had got into the Solent.

But I answered, 'It was bit too jumpy to think that! But we had a lucky turning.' We drank our tot and then the watch below turned in, or lay down somewhere to try and get some rest. I returned to my watch on deck, but, owing to the wind veering more to the west and making the heavy seas coming more on the quarter, we could not make a true north-easterly course for Falmouth. The navigator was a bit worried, and the skipper too, but I said, 'We shall make Dartmouth, what's the odds? We can get repairs done there.'

For when we did get there we looked a proper wreck on deck. The lashings had pulled the stem pieces away from the two eighteen-foot lifeboats, all the plank ends had pulled away from the stems, and both boats had to be made seaworthy. We stayed till the repairs were finished in about a week, repairing the mainsail which we had partly blown away, and then we made a fresh start from which we did not turn back.

We had a headwind when we started, and we fetched over to Ushant again, then put about on the other tack. When we were eighty miles by the log, the wind changed more to the north-west, so we went about and had a bit of free sheet and we carried that wind to the Azores in about seven days. There we replenished our stores and water tanks, and started on the rest of the voyage, making the whole journey in twenty-two days, seven hours. Not bad considering we had a two-day calm and paltry weather, just south of the Gulf Stream, about seven days out from the Azores.

In fact, we and the crew was catching small crabs on the seaweed drifting out of the Gulf Stream. From the Azores to New York we had two separate moderate gales lasting twelve hours each with light variable winds in between. But the gales were with us, and they drove us about twelve knots – not bad, loaded down like we were, fully rigged.

We reached New York. At the entrance the Customs cleared us and we were towed to City Point, New York Yacht Yard, where the yard went to work to change the ocean gear into the racing gear, that had arrived out long before we got there. We were in them in a week, all but the topmast. We had to leave that on deck; with it up in place we was one hundred and seventy-five feet from the deck to the top of the topmast, too tall to go under Brooklyn Bridge.

We were soon ready to help tune up the *Shamrock IV*. We had some races together. She had three out of five against us, but she did not win the cup – too many amateur sailing masters. In fact I have before me now a photograph out of a New York newspaper with the *Resolute* catching the *Shamrock* up quick, when it ought to be the other way about – the *Shamrock* leaving the *Resolute* behind.

The *Shamrock* lost the cup where she ought to have won it. In fact, Sir Thomas Lipton and Lord Delaware came on our *Shamrock* on November 27th, and said he had done wrong to lose the cup. Our crew was the one that ought to have been on *Shamrock IV*. He would have taken any odds on it, but he found out too late. So they decided to lay *Shamrock* twenty-three-metre up at City Point, and send both crews home.

It was while laying up – we were having a rest the Sunday before we were leaving for home (I was below, having a bath, etc.) – that a deck able seaman called out, 'Mr Diaper, here is a gentleman who would like to see you,' so with that I went on deck. The gentleman then said, 'That is the one. I should know him in a crowd! Can you place me, Tom?' For some time I looked at him, then I said, 'I cannot place you yet.'

So he replied, 'I will try to recall your memory. Do you remember in the village of Itchen, a public house called 'The Yacht Tavern'; the landlord was Captain T. Diaper, your father. He had been pilot of the American yacht *Navahoe*. I was talking to him when you came in. You shook hands with me, and asked me to have a drink and I had a glass of barley wine with you. I turned round to leave, and you said, 'I will walk to the floating bridge with you.' We had just got outside, when I suddenly spun round and would have fallen, if you had not caught hold of me, and you said, 'That was that drink of barley wine that done that!'

'Right,' I replied, 'you are the mate, Mr Jeffreys, late of the *Navahoe*. I place you now! How are you?'

'Fine, you are the kind of chap that I have been looking for,' he said. 'You see that large sailing yacht lying off in the bay, the one with three mast-yards on the fore-mast. Well, I am captain of that hooker; she is the largest sailing yacht in America. Now, the lay is this: we propose to come over to Southampton and have two motors put in her, and when ready, to cruise round the south coast of England, then over to the Baltic to cruise along the coast of Sweden, Norway, Denmark, Russia and Finland. I have heard a lot about you from the Yankees what have been over there, and you know I shipped you for the *Virginia II* when I was captain of *Virginia I*. I propose, as soon as I arrive at Southampton, to ship you as my pilot for two pounds per day, seven days a week, and all found. All I shall want you to do is to put me in a good anchorage. I will take her from place to place. Will you be agreeable to that, Tom?'

'Right,' says I, 'shake on it, and come below and have a drink on it. No, not barley this time, but a good drop of Scotch White Horse.' So we parted the best of friends, and I have not seen him since, as you will hear later. Now the day after that, I was sent for by Lipton's manager, to go to him on the house-boat. When I arrived there all the officers of both *Shamrock*s were assembled there. The first words I heard from the manager were, 'Where is your brother, the skipper of the *Shamrock*?' I replied, 'You ought to know where he is, for you know I am not my brother's keeper.' 'Well,' he said, 'you are the one that has taken the three inventories; first: the one suit of racing gear, second: the ocean-going rig, third: all the spare sails and gear not to go. But what I want to know is, where is the round piece of wood which goes on the end of the main boom with the shamrock leaves carved on it?' I replied, ' Well sir, here are the three inventories complete. If you can find it on the inventory, it is in the store with the rest of the gear. For all that is in the stores, I am the one that is responsible, and I will stand by my responsibility.'

'Well,' he said later, 'it is not on the lists. Where is it? I must know, for I have got to send it to Sir Thomas in London, with *Shamrock IV's* wheel and compass. Now come on, where is it?'

'Well,' I replied, 'the last time I saw it was on the ship in its place on the boom end, and I don't remember seeing it since then. Now, remember, one wants the eyes of a hawk to watch the G-damn Yanks, or they would steal the teeth out of your head to sell for souvenirs of the *Shamrock* at the present time.' The manager then said, 'I hold you responsible for it, Diaper, and if it is not forthcoming I will have your bag and luggage searched on arrival at Southampton.'

'Well – you say that now, and I say this now, and mean it. If by any chance I catch anyone outside the Customs' men laying their hands on my luggage, be it you, or anyone told by you to do it, I will try to give him the biggest tanning he's had in his life. That comes from an honest man's mouth.'

The skipper of the *Shamrock IV* touched my arm and said, 'Keep quiet, mate. You will be getting into trouble.' The manager said to the skipper, 'You keep quiet, skipper. I should still like to know why, when asked to race on board the *Shamrock IV*, Tom Diaper did not do so.'

'Well, I can tell you, that when my brother has raced on her three times, it was on the third race that he said he had sprained his wrist. He said you told him that I had to go on the fourth day, but I said to my brother, 'You can say I am a racing man, and that sooner than race with the likes of them that is trying to sail the *Shamrock IV*, sooner than be seen racing aboard with them in command, I would go back to England.' And this is what I say – I could pick thirty-five men now, and have only one gentleman to take the time, and a Yankee to represent America, and to see fair play, with myself in command. I would sail *Shamrock IV* and I tell you I would beat the *Resolute*!' That caused it all right. 'Diaper, I've finished with you.'

'Thank you,' said I, 'but don't forget the lost shamrock, and the luggage search – and what would happen after I got back on board!' Our first mate said, 'Well Tom you have caused them on *Shamrock IV* to look down their noses a bit, and to tell you the straight tip, Tom, I know that you could do it, as I have seen you do it when you was skipper in Germany – I was one of the crew of a boat racing against you. It is as I said before, Tom, you were the top man at the game in Germany, and when they finished having Englishmen, you come back and try to get a job in the same position again; it is like you had to start your life all over again.'

'Well Jim, I am not in the circle, a percentage man.'

'What do you mean by that Tom?'

'I will let you into a secret when we are alone, Jim.'

So, two days after that, both crews went on board the *Lapland*; it was a Belgian ship, but under the Yankee flag and crew, with second-class passengers. The second day out, the chief officer came up and said, 'Your crew tells me that you are the Diaper of the *Shamrock*. I should like to shake hands with you, I am that pleased to have you on board. Come with me, I will introduce you to the captain.'

The captain shook hands and asked if I was satisfied with my cabin and cabin-mate. Well my mate was a Chinaman, so I replied, 'My cabin's all right, but I rather object to having a "Chink" for a cabin-mate.' The captain said, 'Take him to the purser, chief.' So to the purser I went. His words was, 'Do you like it in your first cup of coffee, or will you come to my cabin and have it there as soon as you get up?'

So it was arranged this way. The purser, a little later, took me to a first-class cabin and put a stewardess to look after me. He asked me if I liked fruit. 'Yes,' I replied, 'and so does my crew.' 'All right,' he answered, 'I will have a case put in your cabin, so you can give the crew some, for you should know what sailors are.'

Well it was a lovely trip over 'the Herring Pond' as the Yanks call it, smooth and calm, fine weather all the way. On arriving at Southampton, we were supposed to go straight to the Shipping Office to be paid off, but there was a runner there. He put us all in cabs, and then paid the fare to our homes. After being home a week and getting no money, the crew came to me to know what to do about it. Well, they would not listen to me. They was going to write. They did.

The pay was held up, because the skipper, having stayed as detective for the Cunard on the quayside at New York, had forgotten to send the wage pay book. Owing to not taking my advice, the crew only got paid up to the time of landing at Southampton. But I got paid for three weeks after landing, by only writing a civil letter that I expected to be paid up to the time they received the wage book.

So that ends a bit of adventure going to America to see an English yacht bring the cup away, but they will never do it the way they try; too many captains. All that is needed to race a yacht, is one captain, with one crew, one timekeeper and one pilot. Two or three guests, but no one to interfere with the captain – without he is going to hit another boat, that should be pointed out.**

They were, undoubtedly, hard times for the paid hands, even those who rose from the ranks to take command, but one feels that Tom Diaper was quite capable of looking after himself. The one sadness to his life was that he died a few months before his memoirs, which he dedicated to his grand-daughter Doreen, were published.

One other argument on which Tom Diaper poured fuel is in the origin of the name 'spinnaker' for the running sail which was developed in his lifetime. While some believe it to be a derivative of 'spanker' and others, in the majority, who believe it to have evolved from the name of the boat on which it was first thought to have been flown, *Sphinx*, Tom Diaper had another theory.

When the sail was set and it billowed out to the breeze, one of the sailors said, 'Now that is the sail to make her spin.' A gentleman on board took it from that phrase and reversed it. Called it spinmaker, eventually shortening it to the name of spinnaker.

His father told him that story, and his father was skipper of the *Niobe* in the 1830s. *Niobe* was, according to the older Diaper, the first boat to set such a sail and it was invented by a Mr. Gordon who ran a sailmaking business 'at the bottom of the High Street, Southampton.' Tom Diaper added, 'All this is as it was told to me; I am open to correction.'

45

Chapter Three

It Pays to Keep the Boat Under the Mast

There can be few things more guaranteed to crystalise the focus than the sound and sensation of a mast collapsing. I know it well, since it has happened on several occasions in all types of boat, probably because I have always been pushing technology a stage too far, using rigging which was one gauge too small or even encouraging my sparmaker to go down one section more than he would have liked. Whatever it was, it caught up with me too frequently to be funny but there have generally been some humorous sides to the events.

Back in the days when yacht design was passing through a very revolutionary stage and the names of Doug Peterson, Ron Holland and Gary Mull were on the lips of everyone who wanted a fast boat, I owned a Holland-designed, production half tonner, which, a year earlier, Harold Cudmore, sailing a sistership, had won the Half Ton Cup in Trieste. In order to make mine a touch faster than the others, I persuaded Proctor Masts to make me a very special mast, but in order to make it look exactly the same as all the rest of the production boats, it had to have a single set of spreaders. That proved to be its undoing.

Early in *Go Golden*'s career, we were racing in the Western Solent on a day when there was more than a capful of breeze. As I remember we beat against the sou-westerly with a reef in the main and the number four genoa set. Once around the top mark, with a small lead, caution was thrown to the wind. The reef was out as soon as the masthead spinnaker was hoisted. Anyone who has ever sailed one of the 'pintail' designs that were prevalent at the time will know what I mean when I write that, in these winds, *Go Golden* was a pig to steer. She needed all that I could give her, from tiller pushed as far away as I could one minute to it up under my chin the next. It wasn't that I was trying to write my name in the wake (as too many owners often seem to do) but I was trying to keep the boat going straight for the next mark.

The mast was arcing through more degrees than any of the five of us on board really cared for, particularly the lady for whom this type of spine chilling experience was quite new. Nick Ryley drew my attention to the antics of the mast, which was going through a series of 'S' bends, when a particularly strong gust hit us. I pulled the tiller towards me to counteract the action of the boat and thought I had it all under control, but the mast decided that it had had enough. There was a sickening crunch and the top half toppled slowly sideways towards the lee bow. Racing was over for the day.

Somewhere, from behind me on the weather rail, I heard the lady. 'Thank God for that!'

She has, however raced with me many more miles since then and doesn't panic as we push boats harder and harder down wind and I have the feeling that if ever the mast went over the side, her reaction would be very different to that Saturday afternoon in 1977; it would probably reflect my own, that of disappointment that we were missing more of a thrilling sail.

Thanks to the sparmaker, we were racing again the following Saturday, but this time we both agreed that the mast should have two sets of spreaders. That mast is still in commission with *Go Golden* which has seen many miles of ocean racing under a succession of owners but I do wonder if any of them have ever put the masthead in the water as we did in a spectacular broach shortly after leaving the CH1 buoy off Cherbourg in the 1977 Silver Jubilee race. I will admit that we were pushing the boat hard under spinnaker in a strong breeze, but only those 'pintail' designs would have the ability to turn and face the direction from whence they had come quite so quickly!

47

Nothing is guaranteed to upset one more than the mast failing when you are in the lead and it is worse when that race has something more running on it. Two years after the dismasting of *Go Golden* in the Solent, I was racing a quarter tonner in Scotland. The Tomatin series included the Scottish Championship of the class and I had managed to borrow a production Bolero, a brand new boat, to take part.

It had taken the four of us some time to 'tweak' the boat into being seriously competitive, but we knew if we won the last race with a certain member of the opposition in third place we could still win the championship and probably the Tomatin Trophy which is awarded for the overall best performance in any class during the week. We trained hard the evening before in the 'Islay Frigate' and were sufficiently subdued at the start to miss a trick. We were at the wrong end of the line and had a lot to make up. Nevertheless, in the freshish breeze, we did so and had a handsome lead up the final beat. Not only that, the deadly rival was back in fourth place.

We were being super careful, loosely covering the opposition as we beat down Loch Fyne, Simon Darney watching for every gust of wind on the water to windward. He saw one coming as we were no more than 600 yards from the finish, warned me of it and uncleated the mainsheet in readiness. The gust hit, I luffed gently, Simon eased the mainsheet and we feathered through the worst. Then, without warning, there was the sharp report of cracking aluminium and the mast folded above the spreaders.

Our race was over, the championship lost and with it the chance of securing the Tomatin Trophy. Eleven attempts later and winning the Scottish series still eludes me and all because the mast manufacturer (not the one I have used for many years) had attached the spreaders in the wrong manner, relying on four rivets in shear to take the full root loading. I was cross; Simon, Barry and Paul were cross; to say nothing of the boat's owner who was watching from a motor launch. The only worry I had was explaining to him what had happened – I needn't have worried. He was more anxious to have the throat of the sparmaker than I was!

I knew how the boys felt aboard the four 'Manzanitas', Ron Holland designs, in the short offshore race of the 1978 Quarter Ton Cup in Japan. The manufacturer had loaded the boats with top sailors and the sparmaker had supplied him with spaghetti. The tiny sectioned masts had almost filament-like rigging and the 'rock stars' who had to keep them upright were worried from the start. Then one went over in an inshore race and no one was surprised.

Race two, the short offshore, started with a beat in a light offshore breeze and then a run out of Sajima Bay. After an hour with a half-ounce spinnaker set, a dark line of clouds appeared ahead. With them, they brought wind; no, WIND!!! The fleet was decimated. Twelve of the thirty-one retired, most with mast failures. And it all happened within minutes of the front passing through – the four Manzanita masts went within seconds. I knew how those on board felt but, on the other hand, it had taken them out of the reckoning as far as we were concerned. Just for once, I was sailing a boat with a veritable tree trunk of a mast and glad I was of it.

Maybe Peter Blake and the crew of *Ceramco* would have been happier if they had had one like that, with matching suspension bridge wires for rigging on that fateful day, 21 Septembert, 1981, the twenty-fourth day of the first leg of the Whitbread Round-the-World Race. Four years before, Blake had been watch captain of *Heath's Condor* when the experimental carbon fibre mast had crumpled, 400 miles from where disaster overtook *Ceramco*. His diary entry for that day is recorded in the book which he and Alan Sefton wrote; *Blake's Odyssey*.

"*Ceramco* forges south into settled trade winds. The seas are lumpy but moderate, the skies clear. Last night I spoke to Warwick White in Auckland to report progress, then Jim Lidgard to arrange some sail alterations in Cape Town, and finally Pippa to discuss her journey to South Africa and find out the latest from race headquarters.

We were rocketing along under No. 4 genoa, sometimes No 3, reefing in and out as the wind strength varied through the morning. I went below soon after noon to plot the day's run. We were 100 miles to the north of Ascension Island. Suddenly there was an almighty bang and crash from up top. *Ceramco* came upright and slowed. I leapt for the hatch, yelling for the off watch crew as I went. I didn't need to look to know what had happened. We'd broken the mast.

I dashed up on deck. What mess. The whole top half of the mast was over the side but still attached by internal halyards and wiring systems, plus the mainsail and jib and the headstay. Another section, probably 20ft long, was bent over and dangling down to the gunwale. We were left with a 16ft stump still in place.

It appeared that the port lower intermediate shroud had broken where it bent over the lower spreader. The mast didn't have a chance and folded at the middle and bottom spreaders. But diagnosis had to wait. The top section of the alloy mast, with all its attachments, was under the boat with the wind blowing *Ceramco* down on to it.

There were some shocked and glum faces about, but nobody hesitated. Fenders were put over the side to prevent hull damage by the section in the water. We used the motor – first making sure there were no lines under the propeller – to reverse the boat around until the spar and entanglements were to windward with *Ceramco* streaming to leeward of their danger. Then we used blocks and tackles to slowly winch the mast section back on board.

With everything back on deck – we salvaged the lot – we had only three bent stanchions to show for all the trouble. But we were 2,455 miles from Cape Town, as the crow flies, with only a 16ft stump of a mast from which to hang a bare minimum of sail.

To get us moving again, while we took stock of the situation, we set the trysail and No 6 jib on the stump and quickly were making 4 to 5 knots in the right direction. That was something. But it was daunting to think how far we had to go – most of it to windward if we contemplated the direct route.

We'd been lucky though. I shuddered when I thought what could have happened if someone had been to leeward, changing sheets or preparing for a headsail change, when it all came down.

The rest of the afternoon was spent cleaning up the mess, de-rigging the pieces of the spar and lashing them to the deck. There was little else we could do until the morning. The trysail and small jib were doing their best, set sideways on the mast stub which was in fact the lower portion of the mast up to the bottom spreader point. It still had the lower shrouds attached so we were secure enough for the moment.

The boat was unnaturally quiet, gloom and doom below and the mood wasn't helped by the necessity to let the outside world know what had happened. This fortunately, posed no technical problem. Our big Sailor S.S.B. radio worked through two whip aerials mounted on the stern. Things would have been a bit more difficult had we used the backstay as an aerial.

My first call was to Pippa back in England. She burst into tears. Next I called Martin Foster in Auckland. My news was greeted by a stunned silence. Then it was the turn of Peter Montgomery of Radio New Zealand and Alan Sefton of the *Auckland Star*. These two had done so much for our project, they had a right to be the first media people to know. I had already informed the rest of the fleet on the chat show and sent a telex to the RNSA telling them we'd lost the mast but were continuing to Cape Town under jury rig.

Those chores out of the way, I assembled the crew and outlined our options. The direct route to Cape Town was out. *Ceramco* was in no condition to go sailing to windward. If we found we couldn't sail effectively, we could put in to Ascension Island, take on diesel, sail on as far as we could and then start the motor. This went down like the proverbial lead balloon.

We could turn back and head for Monrovia, 800 miles to the north and have a new mast waiting there. But that would mean the end of the race for us. We would never get to Cape Town in time for the restart to Auckland. I'd been to Monrovia before, when *Heath's Condor* lost her mast on the first leg of the 1977-78 Whitbread. We encountered all sorts of problems and, anyway, *Condor* had been 400 miles closer when we had to make our decision on that occasion.

Our best solution was to continue on to Cape Town by the downwind route, around the back (to the west) of the South Atlantic high pressure systems, making as much speed as possible and having everything waiting for us to replace the rig when we got there.

We were right in the middle of the Atlantic anyway. The African coast, to the east, was to windward against trade winds which were blowing reasonably fresh compared to normal. We didn't really have much of a decision to make. But I got a big thrill from the crew reaction to this discussion. There was no question of pulling out to motor to Cape Town. We were still racing, albeit with our wings clipped. It would be up to good old Kiwi ingenuity to find ways of setting as much sail as possible to speed our journey. We'd be sailing anything from 1,000 to 2,000 miles further. But the trades had been blowing reasonably fresh and, with a few breaks, we could still make reasonable time.

In our favour was the way the mast had broken. We had a top section of about 45ft with all the attachments intact. If we could hoist this into place alongside the 16ft bottom section, and hold it in position, there were all sorts of possibilities. We could still make it to Cape Town before some of the backmarkers.

I tried to wrap up the discussion on a light note with: 'Now if anyone wants to get demoralised, come and see me and we'll get demoralised together.' There were no takers.

Left to my own thoughts, I reflected on our misfortune. Our estimates put *Flyer* 105 miles to the east of us. We'd been level pegging it down the South Atlantic and really beginning to look good on handicap. We felt, strategically, we were in a good situation. But . . .

Then there is the mast itself, slim in section and heavily tapered at the top. It caused a lot of comment when it was stepped in Auckland and there were any number of waterfront experts prepared to bet it would come down. Well, it had – but through no fault in the spar or its engineering. The problem was a rigging failure. It wouldn't have mattered what size mast we'd had – we could have been using a telegraph pole. When that particular piece of the rigging failed, whatever we'd been using would have come down.

We'd had no problems with the spar in 16,000 miles of sailing. It had stood up like a tree trunk, even when we'd been caught napping by a 50 knot squall leaving Auckland for the 1980 Sydney-Hobart. On that occasion we gybed all-standing with no runners on and finished up kicking on our side with the mast in the water. If it was going to go though any fault in its section size, design or engineering, it would have been then.

But there was little point in recriminations. Better now to devote all our thinking energy to getting out of this dilemma in the best possible shape, remembering always that there is still more than three-quarters of the race to run and a lot can happen to the opposition in more than 20,000 miles, particularly in the Southern Ocean where *Ceramco* has been designed and built to excel. Hopefully, we've now used up our ration of bad luck.

For now, we're going back to what they used in Nelson's day. If we can rig the boat the way we intend, and get the same winds we've been having, we'll be doing 7 to 8 knots again. We won't be as hard on the wind as we'd like, but we will be able to steer a pretty good course and reach Cape Town not too far behind the others.**"**

One can imagine the depression and misery that was being experienced aboard *Ceramco*. They had established a good position on the first leg and knew that they must be in with a good chance of winning the race overall (the results of the next three legs would prove that to be the case), when all their dreams are shattered by the failure of one of the rigging rods. Deep down, Peter Blake had worried about bending the rods over the spreaders but had been convinced by the experts that spreader end terminals were not necessary.

Blake wanted to continue the race, even knowing that *Ceramco* had no chance overall, but simply to prove what might have been. There are very few skippers who would have been able to provide the stimulus to a crew that was needed at this moment, but Peter Blake is a very different man to even the very best skippers. He is a leader who would lead in any sphere of activity and commands the respect of all those around him. For that reason, and I believe that alone, *Ceramco* was back racing towards Cape Town far faster than any other yacht would have been. *Ceramco*, Mark II, however, had to be rigged – and re-rigged at sea.

"Not one of the great nights. Everyone retired to their own thoughts, very sad about what had happened. They weren't worried for themselves. They were concerned that they might be letting down a lot of people back home who had shown so much faith in the project. But by dawn we were ready to bounce back and the work to be done diverted everyone's attentions to things productive.

We managed 40 miles overnight in a south-westerly direction. Not a lot, but at least we were moving and in the right direction. Vonny turned on a hearty breakfast before we began the job of hoisting the 45ft top section into place. Most people slept reasonably well despite a lot of tossing and turning. As they emerged from their bunks though there was a fair amount of uncertainty, people mentally pinching themselves hoping it had all been a bad dream. A quick look on deck quickly dispelled those hopes.

There was a 7 to 8ft swell running and quite a lollop so the job of hoisting the 45ft top section wasn't going to be easy. We started by manoeuvring the spar forward until it was over the pulpit and right out in front of the boat. The base of the section had been trimmed off with a hacksaw, filed up neatly and was resting just in front of the stub of the bottom section which was still in position in the boat.

As a pad for the top section, which would of course be deck-stepped, we'd requisitioned Voony's kauri breadboard from the galley. The cook wasn't too happy at losing such a beautiful part of his set-up, but relented as it was to be put to essential use. The breadboard was fixed in place, in front of the stub, by bolting alloy strips to it and through the deck. We then created a system of ropes and wire around the base of the top section to prevent it shooting backwards when we performed the actual lift.

Next we rigged the stub as a fulcrum with a wire run over the top of it to the hounds of what would be our new mast, up over the pulpit then back over the top of the stub to the mainsheet winch in the helmsman's cockpit. We were almost ready, but as a precaution against the sea that was running, we rigged control lines so that we could keep a tight grip on everything when we started the hoist.

It was quite an operation with a few anxious moments, but slowly the top section was ground to the vertical, in position in front of the stub. Chappy went up and lashed the 'new' spar to the top of the stub while Jaws wired up the bottom. We then pulled it all tight with blocks and tackle and made sure it would remain in position by adding bands of wire and big bulldog clips. Midway up the stub, we bound the two sections together with hefty wire and again tightened this up with blocks and tackle. To make sure the bottom of the new mast couldn't go anywhere, we block-and-tackled it out to the sidedecks.

We had already rigged forestay and backstay – spare halyards and kite braces – from the top of the mast. Now we added shrouds from the mast top and from the hounds, using a jockey pole as a spreader on the port side to improve the load angle on the main shroud on what would be the weather (windward) side of the boat. As we tensioned it all, the new mast seemed to be standing well, so we rigged an inner forestay and prepared to try some sail.

Using light cord, we lashed the No.6 headsail – through its eyelets – to the forestay and hoisted it. Next came the storm jib, set on the inner forestay (all the stays connected through blocks to the big grinder winches aft.) Immediately, the boat steadied down. We had power on and *Ceramco* felt like she was a going concern again, her speed potential albeit reduced. The trysail came next, hoisted to the top of the mast (with no ties on the luff) and sheeted to the quarter. The speedo shot up to 7.5 to 8 knots. We felt pretty pleased with ourselves. It was now noon on September 22nd, 24 hours since that ominous crack which had threatened complete disaster. We'd covered only 64 miles, what was to be the worst run of the leg. But it wasn't too bad I guess, when one considered that the previous worst run had been 85 miles, noon to noon, in the Doldrums. The work was far from finished however. Now we had to strengthen the rig to make sure it would stay there and take the loads. The top of the mast was already tending to wiggle around quite a lot.

We may look a bit like a Chinese laundry, but we can't complain about the results of our efforts – 198 miles to noon yesterday and then 209 miles to noon today. I think the euphoria has got the Doc. The log last night read: 'Doctor Trevor Agnew just saw a racehorse run across a paddock. I think all those pills are getting to him'. The writing was Simon's. Someone else added: 'I'm surprised you think.' The humour is back."

The humour remains. Simon Gundry, who received the 'Best Personality of the Race' award for his 'outstanding and enthusiastic contribution to international relations and to the general well being of the crews', and many of the boys hold a party each 21st September to commemorate that dismasting. Since it follows two days after Simon's birthday, the party has more than the odd overtone of a wake.

There was one of those in Cape Town a few days after I had flown over *Ceramco* to photograph her underway with her amazing jury rig. It took the form of a garden party – each guest had to bring a plant in a pot to transform *Ceramco*'s decks into something that resembled a garden – and went on all day. Only after that was the jury rig removed and the replacement mast stepped.

Chapter Four

Sail Free

It is almost everyone's desire to set off and sail around the world. It has a romantic ring to it which is attractive even to the most heavily embedded landlubber. Few ever realise the ambition and there is little hope for anyone these days to buy a 295 ton barquentine with which to realise their dream. In 1936, it was just possible, if you had £3,500 in the bank. Adrian Seligman did and with it bought the *Cap Pilar* to spend two years satisfying his ambition. He took with him sixteen young men and his newly-married wife, Jane, on one of the most incredible voyages, since it was made by untrained seamen, many of whom had never been to sea in their lives before.

On Wednesday, 30 September 1936, the 118-foot-long hull of the *Cap Pilar* left the London Docks with its motley crew. She returned on the 24 September 1938 having altered the lives of all on board. As she left East India Dock that morning, there must have been some heartsearching among those on board. Seligman captures that first day, and the two which followed, so admirably in a chapter of his book, *The Voyage of the* Cap Pilar.

"Only when the gap was widening between ourselves and the quay; only when our moorings splashed into the water for the last time, did we realise that we were actually upon our way. After more than six months of feverish preparations we were at last outward-bound for far countries and the ocean solitudes between.

The tug hooted merrily, the crowd at the dock-gates waved and cheered; we all shouted back, and in a few moments we were out of earshot, and bowling down the river. Now we looked with real interest at every factory and warehouse, the ships moored in the river, the barges with their huge red sails working nimbly between the crowd of shipping, the tugs and coasters, liners and lighters. It would be a long time before we saw any of them again.

As we passed one warehouse a man on the roof shouted: 'Why don't you take some real sailors?' This was the last word spoken to us from English soil.

Commander Stenhouse and my father were aboard, intending to leave with the pilot. But the latter was not the cheerful and enthusiastic Mr Clare, who had brought us in from Dungeness. He professed himself in no way interested in sailing, and was anxious to get away as soon as we reached the North East Spit buoy.

Both my father and the Commander, who in different ways had nursed us through every moment of the past six months, were bitterly disappointed at the prospect of having to leave us so soon; and we also were only too anxious to delay the coming of that dreaded moment when we should be cast off to fend entirely for ourselves; so it was decided that they should remain on board, and we would put them ashore at Plymouth on our way down the Channel.

Eventually, at the mouth of the river, we made all sail, and the tug came sidling alongside for the Pilot. It was already night. The moon was nearly full, but a cold northerly wind carried black boulders of cloud, and kicked up a stiff cross sea against the tide. For a moment, upon the tug's bridge, the faces of my mother and sister and Jane's mother shone whitely in the glare from a hurricane lamp – faces at a window pane – only a few yards away, but already in another world.

'Goodbye! Goodbye!' Their voices came thinly through the wind.

Off went the tug in a thunderous commotion.

'Goodbye and good luck. Goodbye! Goodbye!' fading into the scurrying darkness, like a colony of seagulls upon a rock.

We squared away and stood south past the North Goodwin light vessel. The shore lights winked mysteriously as we passed them by. It was as though they were anxious to share with us the guilty knowledge of our own gross lack of experience. Perhaps they approved of our temerity. We felt suddenly more courageous, more encouraged.

For to us this was indeed a voyage of discovery and adventure. Not in the accepted journalistic sense. We did not claim to be attempting anything that had not been done many hundreds of times before, that could not equally well be achieved by any number of others, with no better qualifications than ours. To us this voyage was an adventure in quite a different sphere; we carried no wireless set of any sort; the *Cap Pilar* had no engine. We were out to discover whether a score of healthy young people could live happily together for a long time, without any contact with the world to which they had been accustomed; with no other tie than a common determination to make the voyage a success. We were out to rediscover the world, but above all, to discover ourselves.

In point of fact we had never had any misgivings concerning our ability to sail the ship. We were all very young, and dead keen to learn. We suffered from no delusions as to the exact extent of our knowledge and abilities; but we felt certain that we could make up for any gaps in our seafaring education, by always taking every possible precaution, even when we knew that an older seaman would probably stand more boldly upon his course. Our determination to do this cleared our consciences of any qualms as to our right to take the ship to sea.

Three of us were sufficiently competent to navigate; two of us knew enough meteorology not to make any bad mistakes. Three of us again understood the broad principles of ship-handling; and most important of all, we had made certain that the *Cap Pilar* would be a thoroughly strong and seaworthy vessel. So we bid the lights of Kent a cheery farewell.

Excluding my father and the Commander, we were nineteen all told aboard the *Cap Pilar* at this stage of the voyage. Jane, myself, Lars, Francis Newell, George the Doc and Allon (of whom more later) all lived aft. In the forecastle were Donnelly, Potter, Money, Sanson, McDonald, Marsh, Roach, Romm, Roper and Burgess. Gelder slept in a small cabin abaft the forecastle, and in one near by was Charles Payne, the cook.

Except for Sanson, none of the crowd forward had ever been to sea before. The youngest of them was Peter Roach, aged eighteen, and the eldest Kurt Romm, who was twenty-eight. Before leaving London they had chosen John Donnelly as their bos'n. Newell, who was to be second mate, had developed a poisoned finger; and at the last moment Allon, our only yachtsman friend, had volunteered to come with us as far as Maderia, by which time it was hoped that Newell would be on watch again.

We have always felt since that the cruise would have ended at Maderia but for Allon. He did more to keep up our spirits during the first stormy fortnight of the voyage than anyone else in the ship. Apart from the fact that he was an expert seaman, Allon's most remarkable characteristic was his uncanny flair for making everybody happy.

The wind remained fair, and we sailed down the Channel as easily as we had come up two weeks before. We passed the tall finger of Dungeness in the early morning on 1st October. The weather was now cold and miserable; occasionally, too, there was fog, and we saw no more of the coast till we reached St. Catherine's Head on the Isle of Wight. The autumn was definitely settling in, and many of us felt glad that we should soon be in a summer climate.

Gelder was in great spirits. We had warned him that at this time of the year it would probably rain and blow most of the way to Maderia; but he was not to be discouraged, and went round asserting that, now he had at last managed to get us safely to sea, he was going to relax and enjoy himself.

During the afternoon of Friday 2nd October, the wind drew easterly and freshened. The black cliffs of the Start came out of the mist on the starboard bow, and we stood right in to signal to Lloyds station on Prawl Point.

The ship was making nine knots before a fine commanding breeze, and we had to hoist and haul down our signals at full speed, to get the whole message away before we were out of sight.

Two hours later we were off Plymouth, where the boat for which we had signalled was waiting to take my father and Commander Stenhouse ashore. The wind had freshened a little, and the white caps tumbled on every wave. The boat came up like a cork alongside. My father jumped. Up came the boat again. The Commander jumped. The boat sheered away. Three hearty cheers from all on board. Three more from the boat; then, 'Hard up the helm! Main and spanker sheets!' and once more, after nearly two years within the gates of the Channel, *Cap Pilar* stood away for the open sea.

The light was beginning to fail. The wind shifted into the south-east and freshened more rapidly, the sky to windward darkened.

This was the loneliest, most dismal moment I had ever known. For the past six months there had always been my father or the Commander to share the heaviest responsibilities. More than that, we had been Englishmen in our own country; but I do not believe that any of us had realised before to what an extent we depended upon the quiet, sensible solidity of England. Now we could depend upon it no more; from now on we must face every emergency alone.

By the staggering roll of the ship, we knew already that she was far too stiffly ballasted. For a moment I wondered whether this might be considered a sufficient excuse for putting back into Plymouth – anything to relieve that awful 'abandoned' feeling.

Lars and I wandered forward to make sure that all the gear was in its right place, in case we had to shorten sail suddenly during the night.

In the south-east the sky grew darker and more threatening. Soon little stinging needles of rain struck across the deck. The barometer was falling steadily. We could see that we were to be allowed no respite in which to become accustomed to our surroundings; it was going to blow hard before morning.

61

Right ahead the Eddystone Light rose slowly out of the sea; then shone brilliantly upon us as we passed, making our white spars gleam silver. *Cap Pilar* strode on with the wind in her hair. Soon she began to feel the first scend of the big Atlantic swells. She plunged and snorted; the first spray came hissing across her fore-deck. She came to life in the rising sea, as though the smell of blue water had lifted years from her sturdy old shoulders.

I went down into the hold. Here I no longer heard the howling of the wind; only the swish and gurgle of the bilge-water, accompanied by an almighty creaking and groaning, where the new timber chafed against her sides as she worked. Now and then a sea would crash against her; she seemed more than ever alive down here. Every part of her was moving inches as she rolled and plunged. I glanced anxiously round; but the sight of her massive beams and frames made my mind easier. This was my first experience of a wooden ship, so I could only hope that there was some truth in the saying that 'while she creaks she swims'.

I went on deck again, and for a long time Jane and I stood arm-in-arm upon the poop, saying little but wondering gloomily what the next two years would bring.

We suddenly appreciated for the first time the full magnitude of the responsibility we had so lightly undertaken; and it is certain that if we had once been able, during the previous six months, to view the whole enterprise in the light in which we now saw it the voyage would never have been made.

Into this atmosphere of gloom bounced Gelder: 'Off at last' he said full of boisterous good-fellowship. 'I'll bet you're glad to see the last of England for a year or two! All you've got to do now is to sit back and have a real good rest. Let the wind take you where it will. That's what I'm going to do anyway. Boy, what a life!'

At a moment like this, high spirits only served to deepen our depression. It was also getting very cold, and soon Jane went below. I stayed to lean on the taffrail, and to stare moodily across the water at the last dark heads of England. All the worn old descriptions of the English countryside came to my mind: green lanes and sunny meadows, where we had played as children; lazy rivers, shady gardens, woods, moors and mountains – all these seemed suddenly to have assumed their original, their true and important beauty. Why, during the last few years, had I never found time to see and to enjoy all these things? I had become no more than a casual visitor at home. And now England was once more watching me out of sight. England, the thoughtful host watching his departing guests, and Eddystone glowing intermittently like the cigar between his teeth. **

From 'The Voyage of the *Cap Pilar*' *by Adrian Seligman*

What a glorious beginning to an adventure for a group of young people in an age of great conservatism. In the eyes of their elders, they should have been carving a career or at least preparing themselves for a way of earning a respectable living. Instead, they took off into the blue beyond and did more to cushion themselves against the hardships they would face in the rest of their lives.

A year after they returned, England was at war, after which the ships were all gone. Their opportunity was one they had to take. The *Cap Pilar* is one of the earliest of my memories.

Following her successful voyage, she was purchased by the Nautical College of Haifa and was taken to Aldous Successor's yard at Brightlingsea where she was hauled out on the slipway, which has long since been replaced by a public dinghy park. Her tall masts and yards impressed this young boy greatly, as did her long bowsprit.

War clouds were gathering and the boys of the Haifa College never did receive their barquentine. She was moved up the Colne River to lie alongside the quay at Wivenhoe to rot. One wonders what happened to those who sailed on board her during her last voyage; doubtless their tales would fill a library.

The amateurs had their way at a time when passage in sail was coming to an end. The 1939-45 war inexorably sealed the fate of the sailing ship. It had already been sealed perhaps; the era of the steamer had overtaken them; but in their final years there was one man who recorded much of what he did aboard the few that did survive to work until the jackboots that trampled Europe to submission, unknowingly kicked sailing ships into their grave; Alan Villiers.

"I stood at a railroad crossing at Momence in Illinois and watched a freight train thunder by. The whole roadway trembled with the shock of the passing; behind the powerful engine, belching red fumes from its stubbed stack into the night, the long line of steel trucks roared by, sixty miles an hour. I had time barely to notice that they were laden with coal. Above me I could hear the brief whirring of the night mail 'plane from Chicago to St. Louis, its tail lights disappearing as it hurried on its way. Along the concrete roadway parked automobiles waited impatiently for the freight train's passing, that they also might speed onwards to wherever they were bound: hurrying there, hurrying away again – hustle, rush, speed! Coal trucks at a mile a minute; letters at three! Beside the rail tracks the ordered maze of the 'phone wires hummed with the bustle of the nation's business; the night air was filled with the croonings, the buffoonings, and the shouts of the radio performers, to be loosed upon the unoffending ear by the turning of a switch in a motor-car. In any city's streets a few cents would bring the morrow's newspaper, rushed from the noisy press to serve the demands of citizens grown accustomed to reading their evening news at 10 am.

I stood and watched and ruminated, and I thought it was strange, in a speed-mad world, that the unhurried lovely sailing-ship should still survive. It was strange, with all other forms of transport mechanised and speeded up, that the deep-water square-rigged ship should still wander along her lonely seaways carrying cargoes, wresting her progress with God's wind from His ocean, unaided by the mechanical genius of man. Yet the number of the surviving sailing ships now is few, and rapidly growing fewer. From my window as I write I can see, outlined moodily in the haze of a harbour fog, the grace of a full-rigged ship lying at her moorings. Her name is *Tusitala*; she has been afloat, under the British, Norwegian, Swiss (a wartime episode) and American flags, for half a century, but her seagoing days are ended now.

Beside her there is but one working full-rigged ship in all the world, the sweet and murderous *Grace Harwar* that I know so well. Out in San Francisco Bay ten sailing ships lie rusting at their Saucalito anchorages and their Alameda moorings. In Los Angeles a wooden full-rigged ship disintegrates in a corner of a graveyard dock while the motion picture scenarists toy with 'sea' films that might find some poor use for her. At Winslow in the state of Washington, the four-masted barques *Monogabela* and *Moshulu* swing to imprisoning anchors that have held them there five years. Nearby the hulks of the famous *Daylight* and the old *William T. Lewis* both cut down now to gypsum barges, are laid up for the want of employment even in that lowly calling. Off Long Beach the schooner *Minnie A. Caine*, once a well known Australian trader, is permanently moored as a fishing barge for the use of weekend anglers. In the Alaska Packers' basin in the Oakland Creek, a full-rigged ship is being dolled up for a poppy show to tour around the world with an embalmed whale in her lower hold and a waxworks in her 'tweendeck, to be a wandering side-show from Coney Island. Poor ship! Poor ships!

In Europe even the Norwegians have abandoned sail, save for some small school ships used for training. The Swedes have let the sweet *Routenburn*, loveliest model of them all, go to the knackers of Stavanger; the Danes, the British and the Dutch no longer show their colours from the peak of any working sailing-ship. The three little West Indies barques *Claudia*, *Suzanne*, and *Germaine* – French owned and Danish sailed – will carry their logwood cargoes no more, for each is to be broken up as she arrives in Europe. In the Baltic the stout firewood barques *Loch Linnhe* and *Plus* have been cast ashore; in Germany the famous nitrate fleet of the House of Laeisz had dwindled to two ships, neither of which can now secure nitrate cargoes. The growth of the artificial nitrate industry has forced them out of business, and now square rig will fight its way to the west'ard round the Horn no more. That bitter road is abandoned entirely to the albatross and the gull; what few square-rigged ships may pass that way come eastward from Australia, racing to Europe with their grain. From the west they

65

come, decks awash and rigging spume-covered with the gale-flung brine, parting the grey seas with their sharp cutwaters, driving onwards with their thousand tons of grain. It is an easy passage that way, from the west to the east with the permanent winds. There are gales, of course, and ice and snow and frigid cold. But it is a passage soon made, a rounding soon accomplished, a hazard quickly gained. The long, long, bitter thrash to the west'ard was a far different story; the sailing-ship sailors of another day reckoned an eastbound passage from Australia as not rounding of the Horn at all.

But to the boy-crews of today it is enough.

All of the surviving working square-rigged ships in the world today could be comfortably moored in one London dock, and still leave room for steamers. They could all find anchorage in the River Derwent in Tasmania, and leave place for the British Fleet besides. There remain only a handful of old barques that carry Baltic timber down to London in the summer months, and the racing grain fleet from Australia. Of the odd score of these that annually sail from Spencer and St. Vincent's Gulf to the English Channel with wheat cargoes, seventeen are Finnish. Of these, fourteen are the property of one old man – Erikson, the Sea-King of the Åland Island, the last of the sailing-ship owners in the world. He sails his fleet on three great principles unknown in other lines: the cardinal points of his ship-management are that there shall be no insurance, no overheads, and no depreciation.

His vessels sail uninsured because of the high cost of covering them, for underwriters have an erroneous but fixed idea that the deep-sea sailor is more likely to become a loss than the average steamship, and therefore their rates are correspondingly higher – so high that, in the course of one year, the premiums charged would cover the entire worth of two ships in the fleet; and so far the average loss has not been more than one ship annually. Therefore insurance would be uneconomic, and that cost is saved. There are no overheads since the Erikson Line maintains no office, in the ordinary sense; Captain Erikson lives in a wooden house by the side of the main street in Mariehamn, in the Åland Islands, and his office is a hut in the garden. He is his own manager, his own marine superintendent, his own board of directors. He is a one-man Line; he carries the risks, makes the decisions, holds the meetings.

And there is no depreciation since, in most cases, he bought his ships when all other owners had tired of them; and the prices he paid were so little above the scrap value that, so long as the vessels but remain afloat, they can never become worth less than he paid for them.

Manning is no problem. It is more difficult to persuade young men and boys – and girls too, at times – not to go in these sailing ships than it is to induce them to offer their services. There are still many nations in Europe which make service in deep sea sail compulsory for all aspirants for seagoing officers' certificates; the only manner in which such experience can be gained is by buying an apprenticeship in a Finnish vessel. The price is a thousand German marks and the term of service two years. There are always more applicants than vacancies. They come from all countries and all races, except the Jewish: a Jew in a square-rigger's half-deck has always been unknown. Germans, Norwegians, Belgians, Americans, British, Hollanders, Swedes, French, Danes, Estonians, Australians, New Zealanders, Peruvians and South Africans – these and many more may always be found. The captains and the senior officers are Swedish Finns from the Åland Islands; the cooks, stewards, carpenters and sailmakers are usually likewise. The official language is Swedish, though German and English are also constantly used. The true Finnish language is rarely used. The Swedish Ålanders have no time for that queer, musical tongue, except to curse in it. A curse in Finnish rolls with pleasing malevolence from the tongue, affrighting the listeners with the very viciousness of its savage sounds; no matter how mild it may be (and Finnish curses usually sound like watered milk dripping down a drain when translated) its effect is good.

Run upon the lines of strictest economy as they must be, the sailing ships find their last employment in the carriage of grain from Australia. No sentiment secures them their cargoes. If the steamers could carry all the grain they would take it. A British tramp owner made a special trip to Spencer Gulf to find out on the spot how and why the Finnish ships still managed to secure cargoes there, meaning to take their business and offer lower terms with his hog-lined steamers. He found what other owners knew – that the sailors secured cargoes merely because they were prepared to wait indefinitely for them, because they could afford to lie long weeks at open anchorages, taking in their cargoes piecemeal a few sacks at a time. They went to small ports – Port Victoria and Port Broughton and such places – which had formerly been accustomed to lightering their wheat to the larger port of Wallaroo. The sailing-ships, by anchoring off the farmers' jetties, saved these lightering costs; therefore they secured cargoes. The steamer, with her coal consumption and her home office and her overheads, her engineers and her radio and her cooks, could not spend five weeks loading 60,000 bags of grain: if such a cargo could not be got under hatches in five days there would be no money in it for her owners. True, the insurance rate on the cargoes is a trifle higher in sail; but the freight is invariably a little lower than current steamship rates to offset this.

There is a gambling element in buying cargo under sail. The sailing ship gives free warehousing over a period of from three to five months while she is bringing the grain to its destination; there is no sense in hurrying a depressed commodity to an overstocked market. The price of wheat has been and is deplorably low, in these days of worldwide depression; there is the ghost of a chance that it might rise while the sailor is at sea. Those persons and firms whose business it is to gamble with such things on the Baltic Exchange in London and elsewhere stand to profit in this event; a firm once profiting by the chance charter of a cargo under sail will look benevolently upon the square-rigged ship ever afterwards.

Yet it is a worrying and difficult business. In London now there is but one man skilled in the art of fixing the charters for the ships of sail; a quiet, middle aged Scot in the ancient and venerable house of Clarkson's of Fenchurch Street, who sits at his desk with his telephones and his assistants and looks after the charters of all the sailing-ships in the world. The 'fixing' of a sailing-ship in the grain trade is a skilled and highly delicate business. There are, on the one hand, a group of persons who grow wheat or who represent those who grow wheat; on the other hand, a group of persons who own ships or who represent those who do the actual owning. The growers of the wheat desire to hire transportation for their crops to Europe, naturally seeking to pay as little as possible for this service; the owners of the ships desire to be paid for carrying the wheat, naturally seeking to be paid as much as possible for this service. Their position is confused by the multiplicity of nationalities holding ships; by the great number of steamships which are laid up but which, should the freight market ever show so much as a hint of an upward trend, would be stampeded on the market; and by the impossibility of accurately forecasting the quantities of wheat and other crops that will have to be transported. The growers and their representatives, on the other hand, are complicated in their position by the fact that they also cannot know exactly how many ships they may need; and they must face the ever present possibility that, at the time when they need ships and must have them, so many other trades will also need them that demand will exceed supply and freights will rise. The representatives of the two groups are always sparring, the shipowners waiting for just that psychological moment when the growers, alarmed at the prospects of a diversion of tonnage elsewhere, and fearful of being left with their grain on a rapidly rising freight market, will be prepared to pay just a trifle more for the carriage of their cargoes than the circumstances warrant; and the growers, on their side, waiting for that much more probable moment when the owners, alarmed that their host of ships may find no work at all, will begin to cut one another's throats and accept freight rates unprofitable to themselves but useful to the growers.

Closely in touch with all this, watching and waiting, sits the gentleman in Clarkson's office, aware alike of the probable crop estimates in South Australia, Kansas, Saskatchewan and Siberia, of the tendencies of Greek shipowners, and the possibility of a rush in linseed chartering from the River Plate. In his mind's eye are all tramp steamers, all tramp markets, all harvest prospects, all

69

detail relating to the carriage of bulk commodities in ships' bottoms from all those producing countries known briefly as 'abroad' to the United Kingdom and to Europe. Up his sleeve are twenty sailing-ships, held there always waiting to be offered to the growers' men prowling the floor of the Baltic Exchange, to be put up for their bidding at just that moment when they are likely to pay most for their services. He offers them one by one or in groups of two or three, as the circumstances warrant; and generally he does pretty well. A bad harvest, a panicked market glutted with empty bottoms, an over supply of grain – these things can largely nullify his efforts and defeat his knowledge. There have been years when the square-rigged ships, having gone out to Australia in ballast in the hope of obtaining grain, sailed back round the Horn home again still in ballast because there was no grain for them. In 1930 only eight big sailing-ships were chartered for Australian grain; in 1931 there were twelve; in 1932 and 1933 however, conditions were better, and twenty ships were chartered in both of those years.

As recently as 1921 there were 140. The other 120 ships are gone and will never be replaced; the Finnish remnant must soon follow them. They are old and their days are numbered, and when they are gone there will be no more. The freight trains will thunder on and the airplanes roar, but the wind will not sigh again gently in the rigging of an old sailing-ship, wandering quietly through the Trades; the sun will not shine again upon billowed sails swelling peacefully above rusted hulls; beauty will be gone from the ocean, and an art form lost to the world.

How soon? In five years, perhaps; certainly in no more than ten.**"**

From 'Last of the Wind Ships' *by Alan J. Villiers*

It was that wonderful attention to detail which made Alan Villiers the most readable of writers about the age of sail. He cared about all the aspects of his trade, not just the sailing, but the commercial background which made it all possible. Nothing escaped his attention, but there was no doubt that what totally absorbed him was the sailing of ships. His personal log would be the envy of everyone who goes afloat for pleasure, yet most of the miles he covered were as a professional seaman.

Villiers and Seligman would have been welcomed to the Green movement of the late Twentieth Century. They were, indeed lovers of this planet at a time when the worst excesses of pollution had yet to be perpetrated. So too was Bob Roberts, the last of the 'Sailormen', the skippers of the Thames barges trading under sail. Bob loved the creeks and rivers of the East Coast and their foreshores. He worried, in 1961, that the right of access to the water was disappearing in many places and argued that the right of access to the land from the water is an ancient and traditional right of seafarers. He also believed that yacht clubs would do well to fight any encroachment in their own areas to protect these rights for future generations and he wrote it in his own particular style.

❝With a cargo of barley for Snape in the old barge *Oxygen* we made our first high water from Orford Haven entrance at Aldeburgh brickfield. There's a good berth there, and barges working up or down the Ore and the Alde (which is all one river really) with ballast, barley and malt often used to lie there. But tides were lazy that week and we had a couple of days to wait for water enough to get us up past Iken; so my old skipper, a native of Suffolk said: 'We'll pull the boat up on the shore and walk up and see the merchant. We'll go up through the Sailors' Walk.'

We set out on our four mile tramp in good heart with the excellent prospect of a pint at the 'Plough and Sail' on arrival. It was a pleasant walk too, a narrow path which more or less followed the course of the river bank, with widgeon on one hand and pheasants on the other – many of them close enough to turn the heart of any honest seaman blessed with a healthy appetite.

Before long we came to notices saying 'Private' and some sported that ridiculous phrase 'Trespassers Will Be Prosecuted' ridiculous because you can't prosecute anyone for trespassing anyway! I wonder what pompous ass first thought of it?

I was a bit perturbed as my skipper, quite unconcerned, clambered over all obstacles and strode along the path like a man

71

who knew what he was doing. I suggested that if we didn't watch out we'd soon be seen and stopped and run in by the police.

'Let 'em try it' he said. 'This is a sailors' walk. Nobody can stop a seaman going by a sailors' walk, not even the King of England. We ain't got many rights but you should be able to walk any river from your ship to the next town or village. A craft might come in from sea out of grub or with men sick and injured. They can't bar men coming ashore and getting whatever it is they need – even if it's only to report their arrival – might have been overdue – missing in bad weather or something like that. People who try to block these walks want their heads examined. Who the hell do they think they are? Some of 'em want to own England and keep it for themselves.'

I asked him if this was the only Sailors' Walk.

'When I was a boy and sailed with my father we could walk any of these rivers – this one, the Deben, Orwell, Stour – yes and London River, too. It's always been the custom, and nobody's ever disputed it until recent times, that a seaman has the right to walk the banks the whole length of the tideway.'

My skipper was right. There were rights of way by ancient custom and usage along almost every navigable river in England. Alas there is no written law to support him and as the walks fall out of general use with the present tendency to carry merchandise on the chocked up roads instead of using the excellent waterways provided by Mother Nature, so the paths are blocked, fenced and grabbed by private landowners.

There was a Sailors' Walk along the Orwell, whereby seamen often tramped from Shotley all the way to Ipswich, though more often from Butterman's Bay to Ipswich. Butterman's Bay was where the big ships (many of them square-riggers) used to unload into sailing barges before the river was dredged. There were no buses then, and the Ipswich bargemen used to land on the sea wall at Hare's Creek and walk home.

Not long ago my daughter and I tried to walk this path and she brought her sketch-book with her. Barbed wire and brambles stopped us at Freston above the Royal Harwich Y.C., a chicken fence barred the way going up out of Pin Mill and at Shotley we got lost in an overgrown morass of broken banks and barbed wire. This is still marked on the map as a right of way.

At Manningtree the other day I asked a wildfowler if it was still possible to walk along by the Stour right away down to Harwich. He had a twinkle in his eye and large pockets in his heavy jacket. 'Oh, ah', he said; ' but you want to do it night time, else you're likely to get pinched. It's all private now.'

Down in the West Country a couple of years ago, I walked the banks of the Severn along the paths the old haulers used to take to heave the Severn trows up against the fast-running stream. The haulers were a rough and wild crowd, fiercely independent and jealous of their rights. And Lord help anyone who put a fence across their path. It was soon uprooted and either thrown into the river or used to make a fire to cook the evening meal, but with the passing of the trows and their bands of haulers the rod-and-line gentry have moved in and unsightly 'Private' notices disfigure the waterside. They wouldn't last long if the trow haulers came back! Nor would any angler or riparian proprietor who tried to stop them, when you consider that householders used to lock their women in the attic and sit up all night with a gun until the haulers had passed by.

Now the barges, schooners, trows and keels have faded from the rivers, the only people who could put these old sailors' walks to good use are yachtsmen – for do not forget that a yachtsman is a seaman in the eyes of mercantile law and custom. There's little doubt that he is proud to be, too. Let him, then, inherit the old sailors' walks, save them from the grabbers, and put them to regular use. Every year, under his very nose, the seaman is being deprived of access by land to the rivers and bays where his ship might lie. It is left to the yachtsman now, for his own sake, to save what remains of another of our ancient freedoms which is being quietly whittled away."

From 'Sailors Walks', *an article by Bob Roberts in*
'Yachts and Yachting'.

Whether Bob Roberts ever met George Martin, I shall never know but I am sure they would have been simpatico. George was a founder and first Commodore of the Ocean Racing Club, later to become the Royal Ocean Racing Club, and owner of *Jolie Brise*, the first winner of the Fastnet Race. Seven years after that, with *Jolie Brise* sold to Bobby Somerset, George Martin decided to spend the winter of 1932/33 as mate of a Thames barge. In search of a berth, he went to Mistley, a village steeped in barging, about a mile from the head of the River Stour which acts as boundary between Essex and Suffolk.

He sought Captain Alfred Horlock, perhaps the greatest ever barge-racing skipper with eleven championships from thirteen starts. He hoped that, somehow, the Captain would be able to help him find a barge on which he could work, for that he saw as the only way to comprehend the complex workings of these huge craft that are run by two men.

On meeting the great man, Martin found that they had the love of yacht racing in common and they talked of *Britannia* and the other large cutters, of Transatlantic and Fastnet races and of the problems the yachtsmen of the day were facing. It took a long time to come round to the real matter in hand but it was finally broached. The Captain thought that he meant for one trip down Channel but George Martin explained that he felt the only way to understand a barge properly was to spend six months with one.

Mistley then, as Mistley almost certainly is nearly sixty years later, moved slowly. There were certain hidden formalities that had to be observed. Some 48 hours after he had arrived in the village, George Martin was taken by the Captain to meet his nephew, the skipper of the *Vigilant*. He had been 'placed' with the family as the mate. After his season as a sailorman, Martin wrote of his exploits, beginning with a romantic view of the breed.

> "Of all the craft which navigate home waters, none, I think, has so much right to our affection as the spritsail barge. Other types have their counterpart in foreign waters, but the barge is unique and purely English – as English as the River Thames. To the artist she is perhaps the most lovely of all sailing craft; and with her sails brailed up, as she lies at anchor, she is no less beautiful than when she has them set. To the naval architect, and to the yachtsman who

74

finds a pleasure in the theoretical side of sailing, she must be of exceptional interest, for in the form of her hull, in the mechanism of her rig, and in the cut of her sails she is different from all other vessels.

Except to the bargeman, who has known her from his boyhood, the ways of a barge are full of mystery; and the stranger to her, no matter what his experience of other craft may be, will find that in the proper handling of a spritsail barge there is a whole new technique of seamanship to be learned. For the time being, he must put aside the idea that he knows anything about sailing, and be prepared to start again from the beginning.

The first thing which I had to do when I joined the *Vigilant* was to study the rig; to trace out the lead of the ropes, find out what they were for, and learn the names of those which were strange to me, of which there were a good many. This did not take so very long; but learning a rig does not consist in discovering what the gear is for. One has to find out what it can be made to do; and, even more, what it will do of itself, if it gets the chance – a process which must be slow, and at times is even painful.

Barges which ply between the limits of Yarmouth, London and Dover have, generally speaking, a deadweight carrying capacity of from one hundred to two hundred tons. In *Vigilant* it is one hundred and eighty-five tons maximum, for purely river work; and about one hundred and fifty to one hundred and fifty-five tons in fully laden sea-going trim. She may be taken as an example of the typical barge in all respects.

Except in the case of 'stumpies' which have no topmast or bowsprit, and 'mule' rigged barges, in which the mizzen is large, as it is in a ketch, and is brailed up to a standing gaff, the details of the spritsail rig remain practically unchanged, irrespective of the size of the barge. Even today the sailing barge remains the most economical of freight carriers; but, for all commercial purposes, power is taking the place of sail, and it is inevitable that in years to come she, in her turn, will pass away. Ships and barques, brigs, topsail schooners, and sailing drifters have gone for ever; and now our fleets of sailing trawlers and spritsail barges are dwindling fast.

When they also have vanished, the hideous triumph of progress will be complete. Of all our splendid sailing-craft and sailormen no trace will remain, save a few museum models and the vague tradition of an art called seamanship.

I say no trace will remain, but trust that it may be true of sail in commerce only. Surely the sailing-yacht must survive, for in her alone will men find satisfaction of an instinct which drives them, regardless of progress and reason, to venture out to sea."

From 'Sailorman' *by E.G.Martin, OBE.*

While barges no longer trade, they are preserved in sail, preserved by those who love them and wish to retain them as part of Britain's sailing heritage. To them, we should all be grateful and each of us should try to sail one at some time to experience the mystique and wonder how two men could work so big a ship unaided.

Chapter Five

The Loneliness of the Long Distance Singlehander

While one may not totally approve of singlehanded racing over long distances on the grounds that it is not strictly seamanlike – failure to keep a watch at sea on a 24 hours basis is not really kosher – it is, however, a discipline which commands total admiration. Joshua Slocum began it all, at least, it was he who popularised the idea of sailing long distances alone and anyone who has not read his book, *Sailing Alone Around the World*, has missed a great deal. My own copy, bought second-hand from Hughes & Smeeth in Lymington, and once owned by one H.Balfour, contains the following inscription inside the front cover:

> **"**A pathetic interest attaches itself to this popular work, in view of the fact that Captain Slocum sailed out of New York Harbour some years ago in the same little craft in which he made his wonderful voyage, recorded here, and has not been heard of since.
>
> He may have perished, but he was a daring soul; no trace of his little boat has been discovered. The question is, will he – or his remains – ever be found on some uninhabited island?**"**

One is forced to remember those who have been similarly lost while sailing singlehanded. Parts of the boats of both Brian Cooke and Mike McMullen were found after their skippers had perished and the whole of Mike Flanaghan's yacht from which he was lost in the OSTAR, but nothing was ever found of Alain Colas' trimaran which disappeared during the Route du Rhum.

Slocum was a man of the sea; saltwater ran in his veins. It was therefore not unlikely that he should find his pleasure there too. For him sailing came naturally, a man born into a maritime way of life.

"On both sides my family were sailors; and if any Slocum should not be found seafaring, he will show at least an inclination to whittle models of boats and contemplate voyages. My father was the sort of man who, if wrecked on a desolate island would find his way home, if he had a jack-knife and could find a tree. He was a good judge of a boat, but the old clay farm which some calamity made his was an anchor to him. He was not afraid of a capful of wind, and he never took a back seat at a camp-meeting or a good, old-fashioned revival.

As for myself, the wonderful sea charmed me from the first. At the age of eight I had already been afloat along with other boys on the bay, with chances greatly in favour of being drowned. When a lad I filled the important post of cook on a fishing schooner; but I was not long in the galley, for the crew mutinied at the appearance of my first duff, and 'chucked me out' before I had a chance to shine as a culinary artist.

The next step towards the goal of happiness found me before the mast in a full-rigged ship bound on a foreign voyage. Thus I came 'over the bows', and not in through the cabin windows, to the command of a ship."

From 'Sailing Alone Around the World' *by Captain Joshua Slocum.*

One who didn't 'come over the bows' was Stuart Woods. His only common ground with Slocum is that they were and are American citizens. Stuart is a writer, bred from advertising into the more cultural pursuit of the novel. It was while writing the first of these, and keeping himself by working two days a week in a Dublin advertising agency, that, at the age of 35, he began sailing. He owned and raced an eleven-foot six-inch plywood Mirror dinghy. After two seasons of that ('At the Mirror Nationals we came twenty-ninth out of sixty boats. It was my finest hour.'), he made his first offshore passage in a yacht. Just two years after that, he took part in the *Observer* Singlehanded Race. The only other thing Stuart Woods has in common with Captain Slocum is that they each wrote a book of their exploits.

Blue Water, Green Sailor, is an apt title but the really green part of it is Stuart's life in Ireland where he seems to have absorbed and understood the proper pace of life. He also found the ways of dealing with the idiosyncratic, an essential for Irish living. Particularly, he found out how to deal with things that go wrong, an essential for the singlehander. He is, unusually for an American, a compassionate person and, one can detect, a Sybarite. Yet he went off across the Atlantic alone but not before 'A last Irish Spring and final preparations.'

❝That there was much more work to be done on the boat became clear the first time I sailed her. Some friends and I set off for a weekend cruise to Kinsale, and as we were sailing out of Cork Harbour one of the girls asked for a sponge and bucket to do some bailing. Thinking that a little water had been left in the bilges I handed down the bucket, but a couple of minutes later, as *Harp* heeled in a gust, there came a shout from below that water was pouring into the boat. I jumped down the companionway ladder to find a heavy stream of water entering the cabin from the engine bay. I got the ladder and engine bulkhead off and found a bare-ended hose pouring water into the boat at the rate of about twenty gallons a minute. Fortunately, a wine cork was the perfect size to plug the hose, and with a jubilee clip tightened around the whole thing, it seemed watertight. But we cancelled the cruise to Kinsale and settled for a sail around Cork Harbour, uncertain what other defects we might find.

Harold Cudmore and I planned to sail up to Galway, to arrive in time for the West of Ireland Boat and Leisure Show, now a fixture of the Galway Bay Sailing Club. O.H. and I sailed the boat as far as Kinsale, from where Harold and I would depart for the long cruise down the southwest coast, then around the corner and up the west coast to Galway, but we began to get bad weather forecasts for the west coast and I decided to drive. We left the boat on a mooring at Kinsale, for collection later. A couple of days afterwards I was awakened at eight in the morning by the ringing of the telephone. (After six months of clawing my way through the Irish Civil Service, I had finally got a phone by appealing to a politician friend, who wrote one letter and did the trick.) A voice asked if I were the owner of *Golden Harp*. I was. She had broken her mooring and was aground on the opposite bank of the river.

I dressed and made the fourteen miles to Kinsale in record time, my heart in my mouth and pictures running though my mind of *Harp* lying on her topsides, her mast tangled in some tree. I arrived to find that Courtney Good, a Kinsale businessman and owner of another Shamrock, had pulled her off with the club crashboat, and we got her onto another mooring quickly, completely undamaged. It had been the scare of my life, for if she had been damaged badly I would have had one hell of a time getting her right again in time for the Race. I sailed her back alone in a Force seven, but it being an offshore breeze the sea was flat. It was only the second time I had sailed her singlehanded, and it was very exhilarating.

I drove up to Galway for the Boat Show, which was bigger and better than ever, and for a last goodbye to the people who had given me my first opportunity to sail, both in dinghies and cruising boats. At the dinner, I was allowed to say a few words, and I presented a cup to the club to be given each year for the best cruise by a member. I was very sad to think that I might not see Galway or any of my friends there for a very long time.

Some time in April I read that there was a second Irish entry in the OSTAR, Patrick O'Donovan, and that he has just sailed into Kinsale at the completion of his qualifying cruise in a thirty-one-foot trimaran. The next day I was invited to dinner at the

80

O'Donovan's Cork home, where Patrick and I got acquainted and compared notes on our preparations. He mentioned a new marine radar detector which would sound an alarm in the presence of radar signals from another ship, and this sounded a good idea, since the OSTAR rules prohibited radar on the yachts participating. I ordered one immediately.

Patrick had had his problems with getting a boat ready and would have more. He had planned to sail *Lillian*, a fifty-five-foot proa, in the Race, and had actually qualified in her, but on a return trip from Ireland to England with *Lillian*'s owner, the proa had capsized in a Force ten and Patrick and the owner had spent eighteen hours in the liferaft, tied between the proa's floats, until they were picked up by a fishing vessel. When they returned to look for *Lillian* she could not be found, and they learned subsequently that she had been taken as salvage by a Russian ship, sawn into manageable pieces and left on a quayside in Cairo, of all places. All Patrick had got back was his passport, forwarded by the British Consulate there. Now he had bought my friend David Walsh's trimaran, *Silmaril*, and qualified her. The following morning he stopped by Drake's Pool for a look at *Harp* and more conversation. Patrick, who was only twenty-three, would be one of the youngest competitors in the Race. Born in Cork, he was now living in England and was preparing his boat there.

Ron and Laurel Holland moved into their new home, Strand Farmhouse, in Currabinny, across the river from Crosshaven, and for the first time Ron had a proper design office. From his drawing board he had a view of the Royal Cork and the members' yachts moored in the river; he could see all who came and went. Shortly before I left for Plymouth, he and Laurel cruised down to Kinsale with me, the first time they had sailed together in two years, kept apart on the water by Ron's increasingly busy schedule and Laurel's pregnancy. Kelly, the Holland's daughter, was a big tot by now and Laurel was pregnant again.

Now I applied to the Irish Yachting Association to be examined for the Yachtmaster's Certificate, the culmination of a programme I had been working on for more than a year. To my astonishment

81

and consternation, I was told that I did not have enough experience to sit for the examination. The Yachtmaster's programme called for forty-eight hours of classroom instruction (I had had sixty-four); six days of practical instruction (I had ten); and five hundred miles of offshore cruising (I had submitted a logbook documenting more than four thousand miles offshore, thirteen hundred of it singlehanded). I was incensed to be told that I did not have enough experience even to take the examination. If I took it and failed, fine, but I did not feel I should be denied the examination after so much work. Apparently, the difficulty had stemmed from a report about my training cruise aboard *Creidne*, when Captain Eric Healy, the skipper, had suggested I needed more experience of handling the boat under power, and that I had been impatient with the crew when skippering. I agreed that these had been justifiable, constructive criticisms at the time, but since then I had sailed more than three thousand miles and amassed a great deal more experience, and I did not feel that comments made a year before still were applicable. At the suggestion of a friend, I wrote to the president of the IYA, explaining my position and requesting an examination before I left for Plymouth. I waited nervously for a reply.

My back problem had begun to abate now, after more than three months of pain whenever I stood up or walked for more than two or three minutes at a time. The lower back pain had extended to the sciatic nerve, which runs from the hip down to the foot, then given way to severe muscle cramps which continued for some weeks. I had been to two more back specialists; one had given me muscle relaxant injections which helped somewhat; the other had told me just to wait and it would go away, and he prescribed a very embarrassing, steel-braced corset to be taken on the transatlantic crossing in case the fractured disc slipped out of place again. Having always been extremely healthy and unaccustomed to severe pain, I lived in terror of the thing recurring in mid-Atlantic. My last treatment came from a quack, an Irish farmer who seemed to be able to 'divine' and treat the source of pain, much in the way that some people are able to divine water. His treatment had the most immediately and dramatic effect of all, although it did not cure the problem entirely, and I was unable to see him again, as he lived some distance from Cork. So I tucked my corset into a locker on the boat and hoped for the best. I was also very careful about lifting things and favoured the injury whenever I could.

At the Easter bank holiday weekend I planned a return to the Scillies with some friends, having been very impressed with the islands when we stopped there during the *Irish Mist* delivery trip the spring before. We spent a delightful, sunny weekend, listening to the local male choir in the pub and seeing Harold Wilson, recently retired as Prime Minister, strolling on the beach with the giant Labrador which had once nearly drowned him when the dog had capsized the dinghy from which Mr Wilson was fishing.

Our passage back was pleasant and fast, taking only twenty-seven hours in a good breeze. We had been supremely comfortable on the boat, what with the central heating and the stereo, and after much work the bugs were finally being ironed out. *Harp* was beginning to be something like ready for the Transatlantic. No serious water was coming into the boat, although there were one or two minor leaks I hadn't yet located; the new Dynafurl supplied by Tim Stearn was working well in its newly engineered form; and with the addition of the new storm jib, which could also be used as a reaching staysail, the sail plan now seemed ideal.

Back in Cork my sextant, which had been left with Henry Browne & Son for reconditioning and correction, arrived, not having withstood very well the tender mercies of the British and Irish postal systems, and I packed it back to London with Harold Cudmore, who was setting off for America and Spain on the international yacht racing circuit.

Word came that I would be examined for the Yachtmaster's Certificate after all, and Mr O'Gallagher met me at a Cork hotel, examined me closely for more than an hour and pronounced me passed, to my intense relief. I believe I was the first person to be certified under the programme.

I made a final dash to London where I conferred with my publishers and took care of last-minute details. Ann and I continued our restaurant research, and I had another lunch with Angela Green of the *Observer*, when I learned that Chay Blyth, who had damaged his huge trimaran, *Great Britain III*, in a collision with a ship, would not be participating in the Race. All doubts about the entry of Alain Colas had been resolved, though, and he would be sailing his 236ft *Club Mediterranée*. Colas had nearly severed his right foot when it was caught in an anchor chain the year before, but he had made a remarkable recovery, and wearing a special boot, had made his qualifying cruise in the Mediterranean with a crew of forty. He would do another 1500-mile singlehanded qualifying cruise prior to the Race.

Henry Browne & Son, when they saw the state of my old sextant, promptly gave me a new one without charge. That is the sort of customer relations that maintains an outstanding reputation, as was also my experience with the Omega Watch Company. I had purchased an expensive Omega wrist-watch which had performed erratically; when I got no satisfaction by reporting this to the American importers, I wrote directly to the company in Switzerland, and within a very short time, the Irish distributors had replaced the old watch with a brand new Omega Seamaster electric wrist chronometer, which performed beautifully. In general, I found that most of the suppliers I dealt with took great pride in their products and were always ready to make adjustments when warranted. Only two or three times in the eighteen months that I dealt with manufacturers was I disappointed by the supplier's attitude. During the whole of the project I was badly let down by only one equipment manufacturer.

My final task in London was to buy provisions for the Race, and for this I went to Harrod's, that superb department store in Knightsbridge. On the Azores trip I had become bored very quickly with my diet, and I was determined to take more time and plan my menus more carefully for the much longer transatlantic passage. I chose Harrod's because their magnificent food halls are stocked with a huge variety of main courses in tins. Any supermarket has a lot of canned food, but the choice of main dishes is poor. Harrod's has everything, from the simple to the exotic, and

I filled four or five large shopping carts with stews, chicken, sauces, cheese, meats and best of all, American snack foods I had grown up with, packed in tins to preserve their freshness. It was expensive, but I would eat very well indeed.

Back in Cork I had less than a week to dismantle my life in Ireland and prepare for a new one at sea. Those last days were wildly busy, every moment taken up with packing, paying bills, making arrangements to have mail forwarded and goods shipped to the States. I was very sad at the thought of leaving Drake's Pool Cottage, and even sadder to leave Fred, but he had, fortunately, practically adopted the McCarthy family, who lived near the main gate of Coolmore, staying there whenever I left Cork for a few days. They loved him and he loved them. It is not every dog who has the opportunity to choose his own family.

Harry was arriving on Friday and we were sailing for Plymouth on Saturday. On Thursday night Ron and Laurel Holland arranged a farewell dinner at their new home in Currabiny; John and Diana McWillian were there; Nick, Theo and Heather came, so did Derek and Carol Holland and O.H. Rogers – all of whom had done so much work on the boat that I could never thank then sufficiently. Friends Donna O'Sullivan and Carey O'Mahoney came too, we had a good dinner and a fine evening, even if it was tinged with sadness for me.

On Friday the removals people came and took away the personal belongings I would be sending to the States, and in the afternoon Harry McMahon arrived. We worked the rest of the day getting gear sorted, had a farewell drink at the Royal Cork Yacht Club, a steak at the 'Overdraught', and got a good night's sleep. Next morning I took Fred's bed, bowl and rubber mouse to the McCarthy's' and made my farewells there.

We loaded all the gear onto the boat and began stowing everything, tied up next to Nick's boat in Drake's Pool. Fred has been behaving oddly for the last twenty-four hours; I think he knew something unusual was up. The day before he had turned up in Carrigaline, apparently looking for me, something he would not ordinarily do. Now after my choked-up goodbye, he sat on the stone slip in Drake's Pool and solemnly watched us working on the

85

boat. I had explained to him long before that he would never be allowed on *Harp* until he had learned to use a marine toilet, and after a few instances when he swam in circles around the boat, demanding loudly to be hauled aboard, he had given up, and whenever I rowed out to the boat he habitually departed in a huff for the McCarthy's'. He sat there the whole morning watching. Finally, we had the last bit of gear stowed, we had made our last goodbyes to Nick and we were ready to leave Drake's Pool for the last time.

We started the engine, cast off Nick's lines and, as we motored around the first bend and out of Drake's Pool, the last thing I saw was Fred, sitting in front of the cottage, watching.**"**

From 'Blue Water, Green Skipper' *by Stuart Woods.*

Stuart Woods finished sixty-third in that race, having endured the full spectrum of the elements. So too did another competitor, Clare Francis. At five foot damn all, Clare is hardly the outsider's idea of what a singlehanded sailor looks like. Deliciously attractive and tough as buffalo hide, Clare reported on film and in a book, the wide range of emotions she suffered from the zenith of achievement to the very nadir of depression.

"There cannot be many worse awakenings than the one I had that morning. As the gloomy half light of dawn filtered into the cabin, I heard the wind shriek in the rigging and the thunderous crash of the bows sinking into large waves. Water poured over the decks and down the windows and there was the ominous sound of water slopping up from full bilges. The *Golly* was heeled well over and I could almost feel her struggling under the excess of sail. It was time for me to get up. People wonder how one can find the will power to leave a warm sleeping bag and get up after only a short sleep, but when the weather is worsening it's no problem at all. After changing down to the storm jib and putting the third and last reef in the main I sat in the shelter of the cockpit's spray hood to

86

watch over the boat. The wind was now blasting across the sea and the waves were grey with long white streaks blown from their crests. It was blowing a gale and from the west so that, much as she struggled, the *Golly* could hardly make any worthwhile progress. Her course was north-westerly but, allowing for considerable leeway, her track must have been almost northerly. It was not a direction in which I wanted to go. We were already further north than I had intended and I was uneasy at the thought of being pushed even further off course, for it would be difficult to claw back towards the south against the prevailing winds.

As the gale continued to blow, the seas built up and the *Golly* crashed and shuddered into the waves until the din was appalling. More and more water poured over the decks and soon everything was imbued with damp and dripping with moisture. Finally, when a particularly powerful gust blasted down on us I could bear it no longer and, crawling carefully along the deck, I lowered the jib and then the mainsail to provide some much needed peace. The *Golly* was quite happy without any sail up and lay beam-on to the seas, rising to each wave until the crest had passed noisily away beneath. Inside the boat, the contrast was marvellous. The worst of the din had ceased, and the motion was almost gentle. Of course we were being blown back the way we had come but at that moment I didn't mind very much; I could only think how delightfully peaceful it was compared to pushing on into those seas. I might even be able to get some sleep.

Before going below, however, I noticed that the main halyard had snagged itself round a permanently mounted radar reflector on the front of the mast. This reflector was cylindrical, perfectly smooth and theoretically unable to snag anything, but the halyard was firmly and obstinately looped round it. I clambered carefully along the rolling deck and fastened myself like a limpet to the mast where I pulled and flicked and jerked the halyard until I could think of no new combination of flicks and jerks that might unravel it. Finally, after half an hour's tussle, I knew I was beaten and before I dropped with the effort, I decided to give in gracefully and try again later. I made up the end of the halyard and gave a last look at the troublesome reflector just in time to see the mast whip forward and the halyard free itself without any trouble at all.

It was an endlessly unpleasant day. Despite ear plugs like corks, I could not sleep, always preferring to return to the cockpit to watch the cheerless scene. I sat there in a mesmerised state of misery, feeling my clothes damp and clammy against my skin and shivering as each gust seemed to blow straight through my oilskins. At one point the wind decreased a little and I galvanised myself into action, crawling slowly along the deck and rehoisting the storm jib and reefed main. It was nice to be making progress again, however small, but I still wasn't sure it was worth the crashing and shuddering as the *Golly* corkscrewed up a wave and leapt over the top. Every quarter of an hour I pumped the bilge but otherwise I remained in the cockpit, nibbling on oatcakes which were the only food I could get down. My visits to the loo had become less frequent but were still necessary every hour or so and I dreaded them, for the action of the boat made the heads compartment an uncomfortable not to say perilous place where it was necessary to cling on steadfastly to prevent a dreadful accident from occurring."

How she must have wished that there was someone else to turn to, someone to help sort out the problems. But there is the real challenge of the singlehander; the need to fight back on one's own.

"I decided I must really cheer myself up, but at first I was a bit stuck as to how I could do it. I couldn't phone Jacques because he was at work. And I couldn't get any food down, although the cook was on strike anyway and I wouldn't have got anything hot. But I could change into some dry clothes, and I did. The lockers themselves were wet from bilge water which had shot all the way up the sides of the boat when she lurched, but the clothes in their plastic bags were dry and after stripping off my damp and sticky layers (the paper knickers were easy, they fell apart in my hands), I was soon warm as toast. By two in the morning, twenty-four hours

88

after it had started, the gale finally moderated and, full of zest, I sprang up onto the foredeck to put up more sail. Five minutes later an arm, a leg and most of my bottom were soaked. For the first time I said a very rude word.

Although I had the enthusiasm to change sail, I was surprised to find how difficult it had become. It took much more time and effort to move the heavy sails around, and the hoisting and winching nearly exhausted me so that I lay recovering in the cockpit for a long time after. Clearly I had to eat more and started by forcing down what was an enormous meal of dry bread, several spoons of honey, a tin of peaches and the last of the fresh milk. Ignoring my damp clothes, I fell into my sleeping bag and apart from an occasional look up through the hatch, I slept for a long and uninterrupted four hours.

The *Golly* and I had weathered our first gale and, overlooking all the wet and misery, it had not been too bad. The important thing was that nothing had broken or fallen off or come loose, apart from the ship's mascot the little golly, who had thrown himself across the cabin in disgust."

The feeling of well being was short lived. Clare had the boat to clear up, and the business of racing to get on with, but it was a case of where to start. The radio provided a comforter – calls home take the edge off the loneliness and the problems are shared. There was time for much needed rest, but not for long. Clare's dozing was shattered by the realisation that what she thought was a squall, was the longest she had ever experienced and it wasn't going away.

"The gale finally settled in from the south and it was possible to make slow progress west under storm jib and treble-reefed main. If the first gale was unpleasant this one was appalling. Not only was I feeling unprepared for another blow so soon after the first, but I was already exhausted from the sail changing throughout the night. And, needless to add, I was soaking wet. But at least I could do something about my wet clothes and, full of anticipation, I went below to search out some dry ones. It was an impossible job. Every time I put my hand into a locker it came out wet and, as I discovered more and more dripping garments, my heart sank further and further. I could put up with a lot of discomfort for a short time but the prospect of being wet for another three weeks was almost impossible to contemplate. Out of piles of wet jeans, soaking sweaters and clammy socks I salvaged one suit of polar underwear and a jersey. These I carefully hung on the clothes line over the stove where I defied a tidal wave to reach them. From my position in the bunk, I watched over them with loving care. One day when all the world was dry, I would put on those wonderful clothes and feel that life was approximately a hundred times better.

The lockers had become wet from bilge water which was flung up the sides of the boat as the *Golly* jerked and gyrated over the waves. But the bilge itself was being filled with water from the toe-rail, the mast and various leaks of uncertain origin in the deck. The toe-rail had soaked nearly all my books and had wet most of the food stowed in the galley. Half my store of bread had got damp and I could almost see mildew growing before my eyes. All the towels were dripping and I didn't dare look in the locker where the loo paper was kept. The leak above the radio was in full flood but I managed to catch a lot of it by balancing a cooking pot in a strategic position underneath. All I had to do was to remember to empty it every fifteen minutes before it got too full and the contents were shot across the cabin by a sudden movement of the boat.

And the movements of the boat were severe. She would rush at a wave, leap off the top and then crash down onto the other side, give a quick roll or flip, then rush at another. Sometimes she found nothing but air as she leapt off a crest and there would be a ghastly moment of silence before a terrible juddering crash as the bows hit water again. At times like that it was easy to imagine that the mast had just broken or the hull split in two, for it seemed impossible that any boat could take such a beating. But with the *Golly* it was all or nothing and I could not slow her down without stopping her altogether. So I left her as she was, water streaming over the decks (and into the lockers) and her motion as wild as a washing machine's. Like a dirty dishcloth I was spun, rinsed and tumbled about until I should have been whiter than white. I tried wedging myself in my bunk but nearly got thrown out, so I tied myself in and lay there in a state of mental paralysis, allowing no thoughts to enter my mind. I heard a banging and crashing sound above the racket of the gale, but was too tired to go and investigate, choosing to watch the water spurting out from beside the mast instead. Even if I had known that the loo had broken loose and was committing hara-kiri by painful degrees I wouldn't have minded much; my memories of it were not exactly pleasant. But then another noise came to my bleary attention and this one could not be ignored. Something was hitting against the hull and even before I looked I knew what it would be. I had tied a sail down along the deck and, sure enough, the weight of water had pulled it free so that most of it was trailing in the sea. Five minutes later I had the sail below and another boot full of water. If life was bleak then it was bleaker three hours later. I allowed myself to become excited at the sight of a clear sky ahead and, quite certain the wind would drop, waited expectantly. The sun came out, the clouds disappeared, and then, to my dismay, the wind blew as strongly as ever, if not stronger.

So this was the great adventure, I thought disconsolately. Gales that went on for ever, wet long johns, soggy food that was impossible to cook, damp books that fell apart in your hands and, worst of all, no one to complain to. Of course there was a bright side; the *Golly* was managing herself very well and was giving me no cause for concern. Also, lit by the bright sunshine, the windswept sea did look magnificent as the great waves rolled across it in endless procession; it was just a pity we had to soldier through them. And there was the knowledge that the gale had to end sometime, although as the hours went by I couldn't help feeling a nagging doubt. There just had to be some gentle breezes and calm seas ahead. Then I would be able to sleep again, and eat again and, above all, be dry again, although I had some doubts about that too.**"**

From 'Come Hell or High Water' *by Clare Francis*

91

Blondie Hasler, whose brain-child the OSTAR was, said that single-handing is the key to a unique peace of mind at sea, always providing that one has mastered the art of getting enough sleep in short snatches. One singlehander who mastered the technique to perfection was Phil Weld, winner of the OSTAR in 1980. Phil had taken to singlehanding late in life and had many reasons for becoming gripped by it. He generally only sailed singlehanded when racing and almost always had a companion when he delivered his yachts for a race.

He was a multihull enthusiast who attributed his success to the three Ps – Perseverance, Preparation and Pocket-book. As a newspaper publisher he had made enough money to indulge his passion with all the correct gear but he had always worried what would happen if his boat were overwhelmed. He had chance to find out when he was delivering his boat to England for the 1976 race. His companion was 21-year-old Bill Stephens, who was on watch while Phil Weld was in his bunk. Weld's description of the disaster and the few days preceding it are, frankly, disturbing for the total lack of drama. It was as if he knew, one day, that a capsize was inevitable and how one of the three Ps – Preparation – did much to preserve the two men when it happened.

"The low coast of America disappeared in the sunset the afternoon of Tuesday, 20 April, 1976, as *Streamer* cantered along at 10 knots in a light southeasterly. The stern, relieved of the weight of the diesel engine, had risen two inches to give her a new lightness of foot. In light air, it could mean 8 knots instead of 7. Both the boat and I felt up for the race.

A new antenna rigged from the port spreader captured the Coast Guard's new sequence of voice broadcasts of North Atlantic weather. All through Sunday, 25 April, as we ran almost dead before a freshening southwesterly, it warned of a new gale center over Cape Sable, Nova Scotia. It forecast winds from 25 to 35 knots and waves to 20 feet as far as 450 miles from the center. Our position midway between Cape Hatteras and Bermuda came within that circle.

Bill Stephens, my twenty-one-year-old shipmate from Birmingham, Michigan, helped me to tie in a second reef before it got dark. By Monday's dawn, continuous streaks of foam were showing in the wave troughs. Time to drop the main. Under staysail only, it required constant attention at the wheel to hold the course without flogging its 300 square feet in accidental jibes. All through the day, the seas built up. Between wave crests, the surface took on that creamy look that indicates Force 9 – over 47 knots.

'I'm rapidly gaining respect for the power of the Atlantic,' Bill remarked in mid-morning. His offshore sailing had heretofore been in the Great Lakes.

Frequent checks on WWV, the government station broadcasting from Fort Collins, Colorado, at eight minutes past the hour, indicated that the gale center, per the prediction, was moving northeast, as were we, but much faster. As it outdistanced us, conditions would steadily improve.

'Bet on the wind's veering northwest tomorrow,' I said. 'Then look for six days of perfect reaching to England.'

So dawned the fateful morning of Tuesday, 27 April. The wind had veered. We'd come over to the port jibe. During my watch from 0500 to 0900, the seas had notably decreased. It seemed prudent to put the helm under the control of the electric autopilot, a Tillermaster, while I took a sun sight through the patchy clouds and plotted our position. I was using an old small-scale chart that showed this was the sixth time in two years that *Gulf Streamer* had been within 300 miles or less of this intersection of latitude and longitude, 38 degrees North by 64 degrees West: eastwards from Gloucester to England, May 1974; St Martin to Gloucester, April 1975; back and forth on the Bermuda race, June 1975; Gloucester to Puerto Rico, December 1975. Like Old Home Week!

When Bill came on deck to take over the watch, we remarked upon the abating seas and noted that our speed had dropped to 8 knots. 'If we were racing,' I said, 'we'd be putting up the main.' But we agreed in the interest of rest and comfort to postpone this until I came on watch again at 1300.

I went below and kicked off my boots for the first time in thirty-six hours, hung up my harness and oilies, and prepared for a nap. My bare feet tucked into the sleeping bag, my head pillowed in the

93

outer corner of my berth, my knees wedged against the canvas bunk board, I felt utterly content. I munched a RyKrisp. Bill had impressed me as an alert helmsman more than once in the past ten days. I could see him through the companionway checking the Tillermaster. I hadn't the slightest worry, only a small guilt that, had I been solo racing, my lot would have been less easy. I took out *Can You Forgive Her?* The first volume in an Anthony Trollope six-pack that my mother had given me for Christmas and was in the middle of the first sentence when I heard Bill shout, 'Look out!'

A second to rise up. Another to swing my legs off the bunk. Four seconds. Bill's next agonised cry coincided with the cracking, slapping sound of flat surface slamming water with maximum impact. Cracker boxes, dishes, cups, books, came tumbling about my ears. Water, sunlit and foam-flecked, poured through the companionway. Even as the mast must have struck the water, and *Streamer* lay like a wing-clipped swan on her side, I still felt confident that the immense strength and buoyancy of her outrigger would be able to heave her upright.

'This just can't be' I thought.

A second shattering smack. Then gently, as the mast subsided below the surface, the bunk revolved upwards above my head. I stood calf deep in water on the cabin ceiling. All was suddenly quiet except for the water gushing through from the cockpit.

Panic for Bill seized me. The trapped air was being compressed upwards against the bilge by the rising water which had yet to reach the level of the cockpit sole. I wanted him clear of the cockpit. He put his head into the rising water to swim down beside me but had to withdraw to unhook his safety harness. Then he swam down inside.

Ten, twelve, fifteen seconds might have passed since his shouted warning, surely less than thirty.

I remember the smell of damp Naugahyde, the plastic fabric sheathing the underside of the bunk cushions. As the outstretched arms of the outriggers assumed their upside-down position, their buoyancy took over part of the support of the main hull now resting on the flat surface of the main cabin top. The water level had stopped rising at about our belt line. The last temperature reading had shown 68 degrees. As the sea surged both fore and aft and crosswise inside the hull, the sun shone through the fibreglass, causing the interior wavelets to twinkle merrily.

Bill and I discussed the air supply and agreed it was adequate. We both seemed gripped in the same icy calm. 'Well, I'm sorry if I dumped your boat,' said Bill. 'But I don't feel guilty because I know I did the right thing.'

'I know you did', I said.

'I'd been looking ahead. I turned around. This wall. Forty feet high. It had two crests just off the stern. I kicked Tilly clear. Grabbed the wheel and pulled her off with all my weight. Three spokes. I thought she'd come back until I saw the mast hit the water. Then the second crest hit us.'

'I could see you hauling on the helm,' I said. And with few more words we got down to the business of survival.

Multihull designer and sailor Jim Brown, who had questioned the survivors of *Meridian*, a trimaran that had capsized off Virginia in June 1975, had told me the key: 'The hulls will float high. Don't rush the vital items into the vulnerable life raft. Save your energy to live aboard upside down.'

From the welter of objects surging in the waist-deep water we grabbed first for the three radio beacons. We tucked them with the two sextants, the almanac, the navigation tables, a pair of pilot charts, the first-aid chest, the waterproof metal box of flares, into the shelves and the corners most nearly high and dry, in this topsy-turvy world. The crown-jewel safekeeping spots were the underside of the chart table and the two bins for cleaning materials beneath the stove and galley table. Here, safely wedged, we found the two gallon Jerry-can of emergency water.

Now came the urge to communicate with fellow men. As I'd planned with Jim Brown, I unscrewed, from what was now 'the overhead,' the through-hull fitting for the log propeller, just forward of the mast and of the midships bulkhead. Through the two-inch hole I could see blue sky. I'd punctured the seal of our air cushion. Would the escaping air cause the water to rise? We thought not and it did not. The craft's inherent buoyancy from her Airex sandwich construction, together with the four airtight compartments in each of the outriggers, provided us with what would prove to be raft status of indefinite duration.

Into the little window on the world, I thrust the rubberised antenna of the oldest of the three beacons and set it to pulsing.

Next we had to cut a hatch through the keel to the outdoors. It took three hours to complete the fourteen-by-eighteen inch aperture. First a drilled hole. Then enlargement with hammer and chisel to make a slit admitting a hacksaw blade. Then a pruning saw with a curved, coarse blade to lengthen the slit on one side. My talk with Jim had prompted me to tuck these tools for safekeeping beneath the chart table. We repeated the process at three subsequent corners. It was tiring, this reaching overhead to saw. Glass dust got in our eyes. Mounting claustrophobia kept us hard at it until finally we'd hammered the rectangular panel free.

Once again we could look out into the real world, and a sombre sight it presented: sky and gray water; squall clouds all about on the horizon, but nary a ship. Here and there bits of Sargasso weed.

'We're in or near the Gulf Stream,' I said.

'The nearest shipping lane?' Bill asked.

'About thirty miles southwest of here the pilot chart shows a junction point. But I think we shouldn't plan on a quick pickup. Let's think in weeks. Not hours or days.

From 'Moxie' *by Phil Weld*

One feels that singlehanders always think in weeks and particularly so as their exploits become exotically greater. To sail around the world, non-stop, singlehanded in 109 days was the feat of Frenchman Titouan Lamazou in a 60-foot yacht; it was eight days faster than Pierre Fehlmann had managed with a fully crewed eighty footer four years previously. Maybe they should begin to think in days not weeks.

Shorthanded transatlantic races traditionally finish at Newport, Rhode Island. It was there, on the morning of 20 June, 1981, that the families and friends of the competitors and the world's media waited for the first boats to finish the first *Observer* Two-handed Transatlantic Race. It wasn't the nicest of days but somehow it induced me to write about it in a different way from that I would be expected to use later in the day when Chay Blyth and Rob James were to bring the 66-foot trimaran *Brittany Ferries GB* across the line at the Brenton Reef light tower in first place.

A View from Castle Hill, Newport – 20 June 1981

The rain beats on the grey stone of the foreshore,
The gulls sit with their shoulders hunched.
Beneath the surface, fish are in their element.
The swallows fly a yard above the ground
Their exuberance challenged by the downpour.
Beneath their feathers, sun is but a memory.

Deep in the murk the light of Brenton Reef
Bids warning to the fools who take to sea.
Above the waves the sentinel stands in dread.
The swell is long, the odd wave breaks,
A streak of white illuminating momentarily
The cold dark overcoat of terminated ocean.

Far out at sea a triple fingered form
Quickens to its long awaited haven
Beckoned by a world in awe and expectation.
The gulls sit with their shoulders hunched
Blissfully unaware that Joy is due around here.
Beneath the surface, fish are in their element.

Chapter Six

Newport – Home of the *America*'s Cup 1930-1983

Newport, Rhode Island was the holiday home of the rich of New York and Boston, where the competitive edge for several years was in the building of mansions, each new one a more fabled residence than the last. That was in the golden era, before the depression, when the Astors competed openly with the Vanderbilts for superiority of status. The evidence is there today for all to see, some converted to condominiums while others have been carefully restored to their former glory and are open to public inspection and to be hired for mega-social occasions.

It was to Newport, naturally enough, that the *America*'s Cup made its way in 1930 after the constant criticism that New York Harbour was not the right place for it with the combined interference of the spectator fleet and the commercial traffic. It was to be Sir Thomas Lipton's last challenge and the first in which the boats would race level, without handicap allowance. It was to be the advent of the J-Class, those vast behemoths which were to drain the resources of their rich owners and force the Americans, even, to form syndicates to build and run them.

It began with the formal challenge of the Royal Ulster Yacht Club to the Secretary of the New York Yacht Club. The letter, dated 3 May 1929, read:

"I have the honour to send you from the Royal Ulster Yacht Club, on behalf of Sir Thomas J. Lipton Bart., KCVO., this Challenge for a series of races for the *America*'s Cup.

The following are the particulars of the Challenger:-

Name:	*Shamrock V*
Owner:	Sir Thomas J. Lipton, Bart.
Length on load waterline:	77 feet
Rig:	Cutter

We suggest that the first race should take place on Saturday 13 September 1930 and that the series of races should be held over the old courses at Sandy Hook as previously.

It is understood that the Racing Rules and Restrictions as to construction and measurements of the New York Yacht Club, as the same now exist, would govern the races under this Challenge.

I shall be greatly obliged if you will kindly cable the receipt of this Challenge.**"**

It was signed by Richard A. Barbour, the Hon Secretary of the RUYC and it was not strictly in accordance with the terms of the Deed of Gift which asks for waterline beam, maximum beam overall and draught. It was, nevertheless, good enough for the NYYC which, at a special meeting on 16 May 1929, had unanimously adopted:

"That the challenge of the Royal Ulster Yacht Club for a match for the *America*'s Cup be, and the same hereby is, referred to a committee which shall be appointed by the Vice-Commodore and of which he shall be one; that said committee shall have power on behalf of this club to take such action in relation to said challenge as it shall deem proper, and in the event that it shall accept a challenge for a match under the deed of gift, then to arrange the terms thereof, and by mutual consent with the challenging club, to make any arrangements as to dates, courses, number of trials, rules and sailing regulations, and any and all other conditions of the match; provided that such committee shall have no power to waive the requirement of the deed of gift that vessels selected to compete for the Cup must proceed under sail, on their own bottoms, to the port where the contest is to take place."

What came next is best told in the words of the man who was to steer the Defender, Harold Vanderbilt:

"The pavements of lower Broadway were burning under the rays of a blistering sun during the luncheon hour on 20 May, 1929. Far above, in the rooms of the Broad Street Club, the heat was somewhat tempered by the altitude. In one of the private dining-rooms a dozen men were consuming liberal amounts of iced tea and coffee and partaking of a light meal. These men, members of the *America*'s Cup Committee of the New York Yacht Club, had met to discuss a challenge recently received from the Royal Ulster Yacht Club, acting on behalf of Sir Thomas J. Lipton, for a series of races to be held in September, 1930, for the *America*'s Cup. Sixteen years had passed since the receipt of the last challenge for this most famous of all yachting trophies, nine since the last series of races, postponed for six years on account of the Great War.

The duties of the Cup Committee were:
To decide on the disposition of the challenge, after discussing the size of the competing yachts and the details of the contest with the Royal Ulster Yacht Club; in the event of the acceptance of the challenge, to arrange for the construction of a yacht to defend the Cup, or preferably of two or more yachts to contend for that honor; eventually to select the Defender of the America's *Cup.*

The gentlemen assembled at the Broad Street Club on that hot May day proceeded to consider the business in hand in an orderly manner. First of all, the enabling resolution was read; then the challenge. I can still picture George Cormack, for many years the devoted, popular and highly efficient secretary of our yacht club, as he stood there reading it to us.

100

Before the meeting adjourned the committee voted to accept the challenge after an agreement regarding the conditions of the match had been reached. No difficulty was anticipated in this respect, and a cable suggesting certain conditions was sent to the Royal Ulster Yacht Club. It was also decided to endeavor to form two syndicates, each to build one yacht for the defense of the Cup – one syndicate to be formed by Vice-Commodore Aldrich, the other by Rear-Commodore Junius Morgan, and to welcome the forming of other syndicates to build at least one and, if possible, two or more yachts. Because of their light construction the committee decided to bar both *Resolute* and *Vanitie*, built to defend the Cup in 1914, from consideration as cup-defense candidates. While these yachts were eligible under the Racing Rules (they had been constructed prior to the adoption by the Club of Lloyd's scantling rules), the committee deemed it for the best interests of the sport to bar them, as the Challenger would have to be of heavier construction to comply with Lloyd's rules. As a result of this action, the Challenger could suffer no handicap in respect to weight of hull construction.

The Cup Committee reported to the Club at its June meeting that an agreement governing the conditions of the 1930 races had been reached with the Royal Ulster Yacht Club, after the pleasantest possible negotiations between the two clubs, during the course of which every important suggestion made by either party had been promptly acceded to by the other.

The principal changes from the conditions governing the last races for the *America*'s Cup in 1920 were:

That the races be held off Newport, R. I., instead of off Sandy Hook; that the match consist of four out of seven, instead of three out of five races; that both yachts be built to rate at the top of the J class, eliminating time allowance; that both yachts be Marconi rigged; and that the hulls be built in accordance with Lloyd's rules, thus insuring an equal strength of hull for both Challenger and Defender – one sufficiently strong to cross the ocean without damage or strain."

From 'Enterprise' *by Harold S. Vanderbilt.*

There was a great effort on the part of the *America*'s Cup Committee of the NYYC to make the competition a fair one, with much attention being given to the Defender having no advantage over the Challenger in the scantlings of the yacht. This similar committee of the San Diego Yacht Club, acting some fifty-nine years later, might well have taken heed of what the trustees of the Cup did back in 1929.

Harold S. 'Mike' Vanderbilt, the inventor, incidentally, of Contract Bridge, was still smarting from the effects of the Wall Street slump but felt that the New York Yacht Club should mount a powerful defence and duly formed a group to do so.

With a certain amount of acerbity and prurient passion, they called their boat *Enterprise*. She went on to win the Cup by four races to one and was no doubt helped in her campaign by Vanderbilt's starting technique. It was nothing like the sparring which goes on in match races at the end of the Century, in the Thirties no one had bothered to attempt to find an infallible method of starting well until Vanderbilt and his cronies in the afterguard of *Enterprise* developed a timed run to and from the line. With the wind on a beam reach, they would sail for half the time to the start and then tack round to arrive on the line at the gun. It may sound simple now, but then it was a highly sophisticated method of starting well and became known by all yachtsmen as a 'Vanderbilt start.'

As a piece of technology, the 'Park Avenue' boom which *Enterprise* sported may not have been all that it was cracked up to be. It was a great deal heavier than the normal one it replaced and cutting the foot of the sail with a lens shaped panel would have performed its function rather better. It did provide an 'end plate' for the mainsail but its real value may have been a psychological weapon which later forced almost all the J class owners to have one constructed for their yachts.

The British boats used a sideways controlled flexible boom for a while which was dubbed the 'North Circular'. When the British owners abandoned this in favour of the American type, they found, somewhat to their horror that the Americans had adopted a refinement of the type which they had discarded!

T.O.M.Sopwith took over the challenger's role from Lipton and brought to the Cup a fresh attitude. The aircraft manufacturer was necessarily keen to use the most modern technology and he did so in many ways. He was able to introduce instrumentation in the form of wind speed and direction indicators on his yachts as well as a speedometer. One member of the afterguard was deputed to recording the data from these instruments. In the work-up period of the boat, this information was carefully analysed and certainly produced in *Endeavour* the fastest J boat of 1934, but it was American guile, in the form of Sherman Hoyt, who took over when Vanderbilt had abandoned the wheel and gone below, in disgust, for lunch, that saved the day and the Cup for the New York Yacht Club.

It was in the third race of the Cup series after *Endeavour* had won the first two and looked likely to remove the *America*'s Cup from the portals of the NYYC. Where *Endeavour* was at a disadvantage was in the strength (but not the numbers) of her afterguard. The most lacking talent was that of a navigator. The race was one with fifteen mile leeward/windward legs and on the first of these the six knot wind had shifted sufficiently for both boats to douse spinnakers in favour of balloon jibs – the sign, perhaps, that the windward leg might be fetched on one tack.

Endeavour led by 6 minutes 39 seconds at the turn and the wind continued to shift. *Rainbow* was lifted, therefore, on to *Endeavour*'s hip although Sopwith was still safely able to lay the finishing line ahead of the American defender. Vanderbilt handed the wheel to Hoyt and went below.

Sopwith panicked. He was unaware of *Endeavour*'s true position on the course and decided to tack to cover *Rainbow* after Hoyt had hardened up unnecessarily. *Endeavour* only just crossed *Rainbow*'s bow and lost way as she tacked, sufficient for Hoyt to sail the defender through her lee. After that he bore off for the finishing line and Sopwith was obliged to tack twice more to avoid the dirty wind from *Rainbow*'s sails! The Cup was decided there and then.

A dispirited Sopwith never was able to put *Endeavour* in front again at the finish. He was involved in a protest in the fourth race in which Vanderbilt failed to respond to a luff. Sopwith, using the British interpretation of the rule concerning the flying of a protest flag, hoisted his just before the finish. The Protest Committee of the NYYC threw his protest out, saying that he should have hoisted his flag immediately and the press had a field day declaring that 'Britannia rules the waves but America waives the rules.'

103

Rainbow was a slower boat, better sailed, which scored a notable victory. It was an often to be repeated feature of the *America*'s Cup in Newport, one which was to continue almost until the Cup left town forever.

When the Cup races returned to Newport in 1958; the Deed of Gift having been altered to allow boats of 44 ft minimum waterline (instead of 60 ft) to compete; there had been considerable change. It was a Navy town, the waterfront and commerce totally dominated by the fighting force. To say that Thames Street, the main thoroughfare, was seedy would have been a monstrous understatement. It was a parade of cheap bars and tattooists booths; bordellos and clip joints; and all this three blocks away from the magnificent mansions, now, in the majority, in a state of decline. Both the Newport Preservation Society, which looks after mansions like The Breakers, the Marble House and Rosecliff, and the Doris Duke-led Newport Restoration Society, which has rebuilt many of the small clapboard houses, had yet to get underway.

The Americans began their reign in the 12-Metres with a distinct advantage – they had *Vim*, the greatest pre-war boat in the class, a head and shoulders in front of the opposition and as good a benchmark as anyone could want. They went in to play with a philosophy that simply stated that they only had to better *Vim* to retain the Cup. That, however, proved to be something of a tall order.

Throughout the summer, four boats contested the American selection trials and by 1 September, 1958, the finals began with *Weatherly* and *Easterner* matched alternately against *Columbia* and *Vim*. After three days *Weatherly* and *Easterner* were eliminated and the battle royal began. Vim's crew were slightly better than *Columbia*'s and Bus Mosbacher's aggressive starting tactics gave *Vim* an edge. In the first match, *Columbia* had no difficulty in defeating *Vim* in a 12-16 knot breeze. The following day, when the breeze was lighter, *Vim* won by gaining the best start and having superior sail handling. The third race was held in a 20 knot breeze and it was *Columbia*'s all the way.

Most thought that *Columbia* would be named that night but the selectors wanted to see the two in action again. *Vim* again mastered her rival at the start and stayed in front despite 35 tacks in eight miles by *Columbia*. She won to level the score. *Vim* led the first round of a double windward/leeward the next day but when the wind freshened, there appeared to be no way of stopping *Columbia*. 3-2 to *Columbia* and still the selection committee was not satisfied.

The last race was to be a cliffhanger all the way. In 15-17 knots of nor'wester, Briggs Cunningham (he who will always be remembered for the cringle in the luff of sails, named after him) took *Columbia* into the lead at the start and led by 1min 6secs at the windward mark. She set a huge spinnaker and gybed twice downwind. *Vim*, on the other hand, set a smaller one and ran true to take the lead at the leeward mark by nine seconds.

All the way up the next beat the two changed places frequently but with a quarter of a mile to go, *Vim* was ahead. Then *Columbia* took a shift to go past to be nine seconds ahead. This time *Columbia*'s crew showed that they had learned their lesson and set a smaller spinnaker and with it retained their lead. They won by just 12 seconds to gain the nod of the selectors.

When they met *Sceptre*, their skills were not seriously tested. The margins were frightfully large; the British design was nowhere near as fast as the American defender's.

Enter Australia led by newspaper tycoon, Sir Frank Packer. The Aussies believed in their ability in racing yachts, although there was little on the international scene, at the time, for them to base their beliefs upon. Faced with the lack of a friendly yacht club in the town where they could unwind after their days sailing, they adopted one of the sleazy bars downtown, The Cameo. They renamed it the Royal Cameo Yacht Squadron and it became their home-from-home, a place where they met their friends and the press.

Packer didn't, as so many had predicted, restrict them to talking only to reporters from his newspapers. They had tales to tell as well. They had seen the New York Yacht Club's selection trials, even had their observers watching them and recording the times and they believed that Alan Payne had designed a boat that was the equal of anything they were likely to face. They had an almost child-like faith which led to Payne's famous re-quote, 'See how the children play, oblivious of their fate.'

What they hadn't realised was that there was more to winning the *America*'s Cup than having a fast boat – Sopwith could have told them!

Packer, regrettably, did not allow his sailors to make decisions; he made them all and he changed the personnel in the boat at a whim. Throughout the summer of 1962, he swapped crews and failed to pick his helmsman, let alone name a skipper. *Gretel* and *Vim*, which Packer bought after the 1958 Cup trials, practised in a most peculiar way; a few practise starts and buoy roundings but never a full-on race.

The one Australian man who seemed overworked in Newport that summer was Alan Payne, who slaved to bring *Gretel* into the racing tune of an international 12-Metre, and only at the last convincing Packer that she would go better with her mast moved 19 inches further forward. The logistics of that exercise took almost a week and the boat was the better for it.

The racing had its colourful moments but all were subsequently agreed that *Gretel* had the greater speed potential, it was just that Bus Mosbacher and his crew were far sharper, honed by endless racing practice.

Weatherly won the first through a combination of skills and failures on the part of her rival; Mosbacher won the start, *Gretel* had a light mainsail on a day when the wind freshened to 18 knots and she was without a full-time navigator which resulted in her overstanding the weather mark.

The following race was around a triangle with Mosbacher claiming a safe leeward berth at the start and forcing Jock Sturrock to tack away. Later, up that leg, Sturrock began a tacking duel in which the crew of *Gretel* triumphed. Payne had designed the first cross-linked winches in the history of the 12-Metre class and *Gretel* was able to tack faster because of them. With his lead halved, Mosbacher refused to play the Aussies' game and adopted a loose cover. Just 12 seconds separated them at the mark and the distance between them remained the same on the next, jib, reach.

Rounding the final mark, Sturrock sailed high after gybing and was able to blanket *Weatherly*'s sails. At that moment the crew hoisted the spinnaker which filled into an white orb that surged power into *Gretel* just as a big rolling wave lifted her stern. *Gretel* surfed down the face of the wave and past *Weatherly* as her spinnaker began to fill. At that moment the after guy of *Weatherly*'s spinnaker broke and the pole slammed on the forestay and buckled. *Gretle*'s crew let out a triumphant shout and went on to lead by 47 seconds at the finish.

That night Newport, and most particularly the Royal Cameo Yacht Club, was an enlivened place. The Aussies had claimed a lay day and even the crew were able to celebrate their win in style. Newport had warmed to the wild men from down-under and joined in with them, swilling beer and singing the most unpublishable songs but it was 'Waltzing Matilda' which was heard with unfailing regularity. It was 28 years to the day since the Defender had lost a race in the *America*'s Cup.

The lessons of 1958 were not learned in Britain and it could be said that Peter Scott went into the match in the same way that the Christians were presented to the lions in the Coliseum. *Sovereign* hadn't an earthly. She was a poor design and her preparation was hindered rather than helped by having an identical boat against which to campaign. Almost any other boat would have shown just how bad *Sovereign* was as *Evaine* had pointed to the poor performance of *Sceptre*.

Much had been written of the superiority of American sailcloth but no one in Britain appeared to want to tackle that problem and left it as the basis of excuse for failure. The raw materials existed; for Dacron read Terylene; all that was missing was some experimental technology in sailcloth manufacture, but no one wanted to accept the challenge.

Gretel raced with sails made of American cloth in America, but her performance was to put a stop to that happening again. *Sovereign* went into battle with sails that just didn't keep their shape. Her record was worse even than *Sceptre*'s and it was just as well that there was sufficient gung-ho in Australia for another challenge or two. The one by *Dame Pattie*, known to all and sundry as Damn Pity, was not a success for a variety of reasons, not the least being a lack of co-ordination.

Newport, meanwhile was under reconstruction and by the time that the next Australian challenge came, from Sir Frank Packer's *Gretel II*, the plans were for a new thoroughfare to link the road from the Goat Island Bridge to the bottom of Memorial Avenue; it was to be the Avenue of the *America*'s Cup. To construct that road, there were buildings which either had to go or be moved. Happily, the planners decided on a protection policy wherever possible and at least one of the yachtsmen's watering holes was thus begat. The Candy Store, where several years later Ted Turner and his crew were given 'gold cards' for life for winning the *America*'s Cup, and its associated Clarke Cooke House, was one of those buildings that travelled a hundred yards or so down Bannister's Wharf. Still there was no Newport Bridge and many's the wild ride Cup aficionados had in those days down the 138 to make the last ferry.

In 1970 there were the beginnings of change in the 'Greatest Little State in the Union'. There were beginnings of change too in the *America*'s Cup;

the multi-challenge had begun. No longer was it the New York Yacht Club defending against just one other club; the challenger first had to earn his spurs by beating all the others who had vied for the position. In 1970, it was Baron Bic's *France* against Packer's *Gretel II*, skippered by Jim Hardy. It prefaced the downfall of the NYYC superiority and the loss of the Cup revenue to Newport, although at the time, there were few who could see it.

Bic's challenge crumbled; dissolved in a Newport fog when the Baron himself took over the wheel of *France* for the final race against *Gretel II*. There is something about those Newport fogs which are as embracing as the place itself. I can remember arriving there by car early one morning after a drive from Bruce Kirby's house in Rowayton, Connecticut and opening the door to hear the doulful sound of the fog sirens on the buoys, the whole of the harbour shrouded from me by a cyclorama of grey-green mist. I knew there was nowhere else in the world that I could possibly be but Newport, Rhode Island.

Kirby was then, like me, a journalist but the design of the Laser was in production and beginning to allow him to relinquish his duties as editor of *Yacht Racing* magazine and devote his time to drawing the lines of more boats. He had set his heart on a 12-Metre but it was to be a few years before the Canadians challenged (for the third time). He was, as often as possible, to be found in Newport whenever the Cup boats were there.

Hardy made a hit with all the Newport 'folk'; the Australian was known to them all as 'Gentleman Jim'. He was a tough competitor on the race course and like his predecessor with *Gretel*, won a race and might have won a second, had not there been a collision which resulted in a fairly acrimonious protest which left the Australian press and public whingeing for a long time. It was only some ten years later that the men from down under began to agree that perhaps Hardy was in the wrong.

Norris Hoyt, one of Newport's favourite sons, who was Head of the English Department at St. George's School there for more than twenty years, and a small boat sailor of renown, once described the 12-Metre as 'a very private sort of yacht.' He went on to add, 'Within a stringent set of class rules, the Twelves have evolved into super-performers whose minor differences symbolise variety of function.'

Somewhat appropriately, I first met Norrie aboard the schooner yacht *America*; not, I hasten to add, the one which did all the damage in 1851 that the rest of the yachting world has been trying to repair all these years, but the one which Rudi Schaeffer built to celebrate a milestone in his family brewing business as a replica of the original (as near as was humanly possible without a detailed set of plans, for in the days when *America* was constructed, the boatbuilder had only a model of the hull from which to work'.

The summer vacation of St. George's School coincided with the *America*'s Cup season fairly nicely for Norris to become a reporter for the local radio station, WADK, and he was also prepared, always, to provide those of us foreign to Newport with an insight which might otherwise have escaped us. He was a man of considerable insight; his comparisons of boats and women were always worth considering.

"Like women, all boats have their particular beauty, whether they are compact or leggy, lean or generous, serene or feisty. But there is an occasional feminine creation whose appeal transcends brains, beauty, or charm – a woman who symbolises some divine elegance beyond herself – a goddess. A twelve-meter, like this sort of woman, has beauty beyond ownership.**"**

From 'The Twelve-Meter Challenges for the *America*'s Cup'
by Norris D. Hoyt.

Women were always an uppermost consideration in Newport; Norris may use them for comparative purposes, others deliberately sought their companionship like Mr. Anonymous who appears in a book on the 1974 *America*'s Cup by Ted Jones.

"In a town like Newport during an *America*'s Cup, where there are plenty of bars and plenty of night time action, there are plenty of people looking for it and more people looking for it than finding it. Such was the case with an executive-type friend who was on the scene to see a race or two and incidentally looking for someone with whom to share an evening. He was complaining bitterly about the lack of opportunity and his singular lack of success, but we left

109

him sitting with a young woman as we went off to dinner. He would most likely join us later, he said, but of course he didn't. We saw him late the same evening at The Candy Store. He was with the same woman, working hard to score and not looking like he was getting anywhere. I saw him the next day and asked how he made out.

'I was very lucky, yes sir, very lucky.' He said, 'You know, I eventually went home with that girl and there were three others living in the same apartment, all of them gorgeous airline stewardesses, and the other three were complaining about there being no action!'**"**

From 'Racing for the *America*'s Cup, 1974 – the View from The Candy Store' *by Theodore A. Jones*

There was no doubt that 1974 was a peak year in the history of Newport, which, somewhat naturally, had to be aligned with the *America*'s Cup. The Newport Bridge was open for business and access to the jewel in the crown of Rhode Island was therefore easier for those heading from New York. It was also a year when the whole business of the Cup did several somersaults and for the journalists there was more to write about than ever before. Indeed, we had a field day as both Alan Bond and Ted Turner gave us daily copy, colourful men in a colourful game in a colourful town.

The summer of '74 is generally argued as THE Cup summer by those who were around. It stimulated Australia's now top probing television journalist, Derryn Hinch, to write a thriller, *Death at Newport*, against the background of the *America*'s Cup that year. Almost as many books emerged from that Cup summer as did when the racing was held in Fremantle. It was also the summer of emergence for Dennis Conner, the man who wore the boat shirts of three of the four defence candidates and was on the right boat at the end, by, of course, being better than anyone else around. Ironically, the only boat the San Diegan sailor did not grace with his presence was the only West Coast boat, *Intrepid*.

There are myths of Newport in '74, some crazed by the passing of time, others enhanced in a way that soft edging beautifies photographs of

110

yesteryear. The one which holds pride of place is that concerning Ted Turner and the original underwater shape of the Britton Chance designed *Mariner*.

There is no doubt that Brit Chance had gone out on a limb with this design. It had tank tested well; the cut-off, stepped back end displaying the characteristics of a boat with a much longer waterline length (and it must be remembered that the ultimate speed of a displacement craft is proportional to the waterline length). There can be no doubting also, that once seen it was bound to attract attention. It must also be remembered that, in 1974, there was no hiding the underwater shapes of these boats, as they came out of the water all too infrequently and by the time their shapes were revealed, there was nothing anyone could do about it. Brit's boat, however, suffered.

The outcome, when *Mariner* failed to perform, was that she went back to Bob Derecktor, who built her, for underwater alterations – the fast-back stern being eliminated. Chance blamed Turner, who he said was no good and that he had no real talent and that all his previous successes had been the result of a lack of opposition. Turner blamed Chance for giving him a slow boat and legend would have it that before the summer was over, there was a one-sided exchange that went something like this (at least, according to Ted Jones in his book):

Turner: 'Brit, do you know why there are no fish with square tails? Because all the pointed tail fish caught them and ate them.'

After which, Turner is reputed to have walked a few paces and made the utterance for which he is famous. 'Even shit's pointed at both ends.'

At the risk of destroying the legend in the search for truth, I refer to the book *The Grand Gesture* by Roger Vaughan, described by no less an authority than Walter Cronkite as 'a superb reporter', wherein one finds, documented as having taken place on 7 June, the following as the entire crew, including a reluctant Turner, were wet-sanding the bottom of *Mariner*.

"Topic one consisted of discussions of the previous evening's adventure in New York City, an adventure centred around the Forty-second Street area. Topic two was the shape of *Mariner*.

'Hey,' Dennis Conner said. 'Have you ever seen a dolphin or any fish with a square tail?'

111

'We're going to have a button made, maybe T-shirts too, for after the June twenty-fourth trials,'

Bunky (Helfrich) said. 'They are going to say, "Take it off, take it all off."'

'If we can't get the boat going,' Turner said, 'what we have to do is paint it white and make a false bow and stern like the old pocket battleships did. Then when we lose we can strap them on so no one will know who we are and we can slink away.'

'Maybe we should paint the boat black and call her *Black Cloud.*'

Legare Van Ness stopped sanding, waited for a quiet moment, and said, 'Even a turd is tapered.'❞

From 'The Grand Gesture' *by Roger Vaughan.*

Conner moved in a mysterious way, his wonders to perform. He was recruited to the *America*'s Cup by Turner to be his tactician and Jim Lipscomb's film of that summer caught one of the magical moments of the two working together when *Mariner* met *Intrepid* for the first time. It went something like this.

Turner, with the help of Conner, had put *Mariner* to weather at the start and Conner is watching the movement of *Intrepid* relative to their boat.

Turner: after a minute: 'How're we doin'?'
Conner: 'They're pointing higher.'
Turner: musingly; 'Pointing higher?'
Conner: '. . . and footing faster.'
Turner: 'Pointing higher and footing faster;
(pause) its going to be a long summer.'

In one way it was a long summer, but for Turner it became prematurely short. Conner was given the job of skippering *Valiant*, *Mariner*'s trial horse, and this was undeniably a trial for the major role. The syndicate, establishment to the core, could find little right in Turner (in the same way that he could find little right in *Mariner*) and exercised its right to swap

112

skippers. For Turner the demotion was almost catastrophic; for Conner the promotion was just another step forward.

Valiant was the first to be eliminated and when *Mariner* went, Conner became available to the *Courageous* syndicate, which snapped him up and used him as a pawn in the sacking of Bob Bavier, the original skipper of the ultimate defender, when replacing him with Ted Hood, whose presence in Newport was only made possible by the ill luck of having his one-tonner aboard a freighter which lost its propeller as it began to take his yacht to the One Ton Cup in Torquay.

Had Turner known what was going to happen, his one-tonner, *Lightnin'*, would have been at that World Championship and might easily have won.

Conner joined the afterguard of *Courageous* as starting helmsman and tactician. That announcement was followed by a letter of protest from Alan Bond who insisted that Conner would adopt 'rodeo tactics' at the start and be a danger to the safety of the Australian crew. It was a smart piece of gamesmanship to protect Jim Hardy, Bond's skipper, but, somewhat naturally, it failed to displace Conner.

Before the 12-Metres had the run of Newport that summer, there had been the biennial start of the Bermuda Race and the ancillary Onion Patch series. Ocean racing then was a far more comfortable affair but it did involve the 'stars' of the sport. I was busying myself with this, sailing on *Oyster* as part of the British team. Somehow, my path always seemed to cross with that of Tom Blackaller and always it was a pleasurable experience. More often than not, it was in the 'Black Pearl' and one had to be in there early, even in those days, to have some tenure before the place was full and a member of the staff was put on the door to keep the numbers limited to those allowed by the Fire Department.

One night, the pair of us were swapping lies with Jim Hardy and trying to cut the lunch of Jesse Phillips, who was there with one of the twin blond companions, the other on loan for the night to one of Phillips' *Charisma* crew for services beyond the call of duty. The three-way attack soon had Phillips leaving the saloon with the blond in tow while we returned to our discussion of how well Bond's *Southern Cross* would do.

At the time, Jim was the skipper of the Australian boat's trial horse, *Gretel II*, and John Cuneo had the wheel of *Southern Cross*, the first 12-Metre to have been constructed in aluminium. We speculated on Jim's chances of taking over the major role. 'No chance of that,' said Hardy, 'Cuneo is a gold medalist and the reflection of that dazzles Bondy.'

Both Tom and I persisted with the argument in favour of our friend on the grounds that his experience in 12-Metres and the Cup itself would eventually pave the way for the change. Jim was adamant that Cuneo would stay in charge. I was certain that the change would come, certain enough to make a wager with Jim. I was prepared to put a case of Dow's 1963 Vintage Port against a case of Hardy's own firm's Show Port of a similarly good year. History has it that I won, but some nineteen years after the bet was struck, I am still awaiting that case of port. Perhaps Jim is looking after it so that it will appear only when perfect!

Tom and I had not long gone for Bermuda when Jim took over behind the wheel of *Southern Cross* and when we came back, I took to watching the trials from a boat chartered by the Australian press. I went along free, since they felt they could bounce ideas on me and also get a 'Pommie's' view for their copy on anything that happened. As a freelancer, the situation suited me fine and they were a great bunch to be with. Derryn Hinch was one of them and he used an incident aboard that boat in his thriller. For me there was more to it than his description and another, almost more memorable, incident which followed as part of it. Derryn's narrative is, however, fairly accurate – fact seeping into fiction.

"Aboard the *Hel-Cat* he finished his running story, wishing there was some excitement to report – like the helicopter that crashed right on the course during the first race of the French-Australian elimination series.

The chopper had gone down about 100 metres from his private press boat. It had made a mid-air turn, then spiralled crazily into the water right in the middle of the spectator fleet. It had gone in upside down and the black rubber pontoons bobbed in the water. One of the *Southern Cross* escort boats was first to the disaster but its attempts at a rescue were hampered by spectator boats carrying sozzled passengers who seemed to regard the drama as an added fillip to the entertainment.

Andy White, a reserve Australian crewman, dived overboard and managed to drag the pilot from the water-filled perspex death bubble. One man who did not survive was also hauled from the wreckage and his water-logged body draped over an upturned pontoon as the race went on. There was almost a feeling that the incident was, unfairly, casting a pall on the picnic. How could cameramen get good shots of the race from the Goodyear blimp with a corpse bobbing in-frame?**"**

From 'Death at Newport' *by Derryn Hinch.*

Hinch, in fiction, sums up the overall feeling well but there was one further act which would add to the general cynicism, but every time I think of it, I have to smile.

One of the Australian journalists aboard was Piers Akerman, a man in the pay of Rupert Murdoch. Piers has since scaled high in the Murdoch Empire but then had far to go. He was, however, a newsman through and through. It transpired that as the stricken helicopter was on its way down, one of those on board had turned his camera towards it and released the shutter a couple of times. That information was like manna to Piers but he was in a predicament. While the film was readily made available to him, he was some 10 miles offshore and there was no hope in getting it to the Murdoch processor and into the papers in time.

Piers looked around and spotted Frank Lawson, the Press Association photographer and a deadly rival, in his own sleek, fast powerboat and hailed him over. Piers explained to Frank that he had a medical condition but had left the requisite medication ashore. Was there, asked Piers, any possibility of Frank helping out. Frank, New England conservative to the core, had no hesitation in running Piers back to Newport, where the Australian quickly had the film processed and the prints on the wire. Frank returned to the race course and it wasn't until sometime that evening that he learned the awful truth of how his good nature had been imposed upon. He was furious and scoured Newport for Piers to demand an apology. It wasn't a pretty confrontation. Piers had been celebrating and telling everyone of his scoop and the part Frank had played in it. Frank never did get even.

Once the Cup races began in earnest; after Baron Bich had been lost in the fog during the last race between *France* and *Southern Cross*; the

115

members of the Fourth Estate were all to ride the appropriately named *Hel-Cat* to watch the matches. The *Hel-Cat* was a red, rusty, steel fishing catamaran, skippered by George Glas, a man with little respect for the New York Yacht Club, which had employed him and his vessel for the purpose of taking the press to sea. Everybody who laid pen to paper, sometime that summer gave another description to the *Hel-Cat*. Its ride was compared to that of a sled over cobbles; its persona to that of the Ugly Duckling in Swan Lake; and its appearance to a half-tide rock in a breeze of wind.

It was probably perfect for what the NYYC thought of the press. We grew to love her and her Captain in a perverse sort of way but if anyone were to offer a can of Narragansett beer, I doubt whether there would be a taker among those who braved the *Hel-Cat* in 1974. We were not to know that she and George were to be our ride for two more *America*'s Cups.

There was a rivalry aboard that boat between the reporters of the two Washington dailies; Judy Lawson of the *Post* and Duncan Spencer of the *Star-News*. Their professional rivalry was as intense as their personal relationship; none of us could ever quite know what was likely to happen next, except that Judy never quite aligned herself to the peculiar motion of the *Hel-Cat*. It was that, one day, which led Duncan to enter the seedy saloon, where of necessity we were drinking Narragansett beer, to announce that, 'The *Washington Post* is walking around the deck trying not to be seasick, but I don't think the effort will succeed.' He was stunningly correct.

When *Courageous* defeated *Southern Cross* in four straight races, we were none of us surprised. We were not even surprised when Bond sailed aboard his boat in one race, as a grinder, and almost had to be helped off. Only the speed with which Newport returned to normal provided any shock. Thirty-six hours after the last Cup race was completed, it was difficult to know that there had been any excitement in the town; all that was left were the memories.

Three years later, it was Ted Turner who caused the upset (or several) but there wasn't quite the feeling running abroad in Newport. It might have been that there was a new intensity in the air, an intensity derived from the West Coast push to be the defender. It might just as easily have been due to the presence of four potential challengers. It might just have been that everyone involved in the Cup, with the possible exception of Ted Turner, who had a no-cut contract, was covering their ass (to use an Americanism) in an effort to keep their job.

Turner's big upsets came from the things he didn't like. He didn't like the 'Beat the Mouth' badges, neither did he like the exclusivity that Lowell North put on the sails his company made and kept for *Enterprise*. Above all, he hated playing second fiddle in his syndicate to Ted Hood. He had arranged (and paid for) his place as skipper of *Courageous*. That, and that only, was assured but what annoyed him was that Hood had a spare mast for *Independence* while he didn't and that Hood had new sails when he wanted them and he couldn't have a choice (except when he paid for them under a private arrangement).

Then there was the matter of the odd outburst, the first of which went on at the Spouting Rock Beach Association, a private beach club better known as Bailey's Beach. On 2 July, Turner and his wife Janie had been invited to cocktails at the house of fellow Atlantans and were afterwards to go to dinner with them at Bailey's Beach. There had been several crossed wires in this arrangement as the Turners didn't know their hosts. It transpired that the host and hostess were hell-bent celebrity collectors who had invited a substantial party to see them parade Ted and Janie as guests. Ted was bored and when bored he tends to drink to excess. Not that excess in his case amounts to much; even he will admit that he is a two-pot screamer.

Soon however, Ted's attention was taken by a well painted lady in the company of a much older man. Engaging her in conversation, Turner found out that she was anything but satisfied! Just before he left, in order to go home to watch the Atlanta Braves on television, Turner remarked about the lady's problem openly at the dinner table. His hostess seemed mildly outraged but more upset that Turner had left her party early.

One wonders how she would have felt to know that her husband made a pass at Janie Turner later that evening. Lee Loomis, the syndicate head with whom Turner was at constant loggerheads, was almost speechless with rage when he heard about the incident, which by then had been blown up beyond all proportion. He insisted that Turner should write a letter of apology to Bailey's Beach.

Turner's letter was one of apology for his bothersome behaviour because, 'I certainly did have a couple of drinks too many that Saturday night.'

The reply from John Winslow, the President of Bailey's Beach, was a masterly work, absolving Turner from any thoughts he may have had that he had caused any distress to the members. He added that it reminded him of a story about President Lincoln and his cabinet. He wrote-

> **"**Several cabinet ministers complained that General Grant drank too much. After thinking for a few minutes President Lincoln replied, 'Find out the brand of whiskey he drinks and give it to the other Generals.'
>
> We do hope that you realise that you and your lovely wife and children are always welcome at the Beach.**"**

In his fight with Loomis, it was game and set to Turner, the match would have to wait.

His fight with Lowell North for not supplying *Courageous* with sails was a much more bitter affair which threatened to spring to a head at the *Independence/Courageous* party. Crew members from both *Courageous* and *Enterprise* were poised to keep the two apart. The irony of it all was brought home by Kay North, Lowell's wife, who said that she thought it was impossible to obtain better publicity than Turner demanding, from a Hood camp, that he be supplied North sails.

It was Turner's contention that in that Hood camp, he was getting short shrift. Strangely, North was the one to feel the axe. He was sacked as the skipper of *Enterprise* when the boat failed to perform and was replaced by Malin Burnham. That move came late and it was Turner who upset the establishment by winning the trials and defending the Cup but pleasing them by doing it successfully.

No one will ever forget Turner in his moment of triumph. All the pressures of the summer flowed from him as he made his way from Bannister's Wharf to the Armory for the press conference. The Swedes had generously presented him with a bottle of Aquavit and Ted's triumphal march was with the support of two policemen. His appearance on stage was brief and included falling backwards off his chair; reappearing with cigar and bottle in either hand to the cheers of the assembled multitude. On that day, everyone, Lee Loomis included, was prepared to forgive Turner everything.

By 1980 a more serious view was taken of defending the *America*'s Cup, not one must add by Turner, who returned with the same boat and the same crew and declared that Dennis Conner was spoiling it for everyone else by practising too much. True to the title of his own book, Conner left himself no excuse to lose. Turner and his crew were simply no match for Conner but they did have one trump to play.

David Ray, the owner of the Candy Store, had awarded them all 'Gold Cards' for winning in 1977 and on a day when they were confined to shore (between broken masts), the *Courageous* crew took advantage of the free drinking at their favourite watering hole and gave it a nudge of earth shattering proportions. It was a high point of a sombre summer.

There was that magic moment or two when Jim Hardy took *Australia* ahead of *Freedom*. The first of them brought jubilation to a pair of Aussies aboard the *Hel-Cat* and must have brought tears to the eyes of their radio station manager back in Brisbane. Phil, whose birthday it was, and Zed began the day by encouraging others to join them in a game of Two Up – a simple gambling exercise where two pennies placed on a flat stick are spun from it into the air and the bets are laid for whether they will fall two heads, two tails or a tail and a head. It's a real cerebral game!

The game was played on the upper deck, even through the starting routine and on the beginning of the first beat until someone called out that *Australia* had crossed ahead of *Freedom*. The stick and pennies went over the side and the cheering began in earnest. Feeling dry, Zed sent Phil for some tinnies (Narragansett had given way to a more palatable brand this year) and Hardy was verbally encouraged by the pair all the way to the windward mark.

In the light airs, *Australia* was quicker than *Freedom* and she finished ahead to give Hardy his second ever win in *America*'s Cup races. Phil had nominated this in the press boat sweepstake and was nearest to guessing the winning margin. A hundred or so dollars were his, but not for long. His winnings were invested at the bar and everyone invited to join the two Australians in toasting 'their mates, the winners.'

It takes some time for the *Hel-Cat* to return to the dock and by the time she did that evening, Phil and Zed were leading the singing and a touched flushed with the celebrations. It was then that Zed, the on-air reporter, realised that he had all but lost his voice! I would have given quids to have listened to his efforts as he could only speak in a highly controlled manner and here he was, trying to tell the citizens of Brisbane of the most exciting moment of Cup racing for ten years.

It couldn't last however. The bendy top mast, whose design Ben Lexcen had unashamedly lifted from Ian Howlett's *Lionheart*, was a last minute addition to *Australia* and the mainsails did not fit at all well. In anything of a breeze, Conner's greater preparation paid huge dividends and the Cup was firm on its plinth in the octagonal room of the New York Yacht Club.

It seemed to us all that forever the *status quo* would be maintained. The only argument against it was that there were to be more challengers than defenders in the trials for 1983. The tide was beginning to turn against the NYYC and the Cup was ripe for change. The only retrograde step, in many minds, was that the Cup would go from Newport – others argued, similarly, that it was high time that it did.

The serious approach which Conner had displayed with the *Freedom* campaign, and its resultant success, was an object lesson to those who hoped to take the Cup away, just as it had been to Turner. The next group on the block knew exactly what they were up against – beat Dennis Conner and the Cup was yours.

Australia sent three challenges; one short of money but not lacking talent or a sense of humour. Alan Payne had been asked to design a radical boat; and that he certainly did; while Iain Murray was condemned to sail her. The six time world eighteen-foot skiff champion found it beyond him and *Advance* lost most of her races. The crew painted the first foot of her bow black, arguing that all dogs had wet black noses!

Alan Bond had the choice of boats, *Challenge 12* or *Australia II*. Ben Lexcen had designed him a traditional inspired 12-Metre and then a radical one. They had sparred together in Melbourne and *Challenge 12* had her fair share of success but Bond argued that if the American stranglehold was to be broken, it could only be broken by a boat which was seriously different from theirs.

Conner was known to be progressing the line which had been traditionally successful and while John Bertrand may have had initial reservations when he first saw Ben's drawings, it was a visit to the testing tanks in Holland which swayed him to his boss's thinking. *Australia II* was a 'fighter' and *Challenge 12* a 'bomber'. The short, light displacement 12-

Metre could tack faster and accelerate quicker than any of her class before or since. Conner made one effort only in that direction but *Magic* accepted too many penalties to be successful, so Dennis went back to the 55,500 lb Twelve that had proved to be the way to go for many years.

The American effort in 1983 was weak. Conner was their strength but he had no support within his own camp to make *Liberty* a faster boat. *Freedom* wasn't sufficiently up-graded to make *Liberty* have to go faster still. In the other camp, the management was nothing short of disastrous. Tom Blackaller and Gary Jobson were the driver and shot caller of *Defender*, the Dave Pedrick design; John Kolius and the other John Bertrand were aboard *Courageous*. *Defender* ran into a series of problems of rating which necessitated a 'tummy tuck' surgical operation to her aluminium hull and that, more perhaps than anything, did nothing for the morale of her crew. That downturn was aggravated by the management giving all the new sails to *Courageous*, their second-string boat. It resulted in *Defender* being the first to be eliminated and the nine-year-old *Courageous* having to face *Liberty* for the honour of defending the Cup.

It was a one-way affair despite some underdog activity worthy of the name. Meanwhile, 'Keelgate' was making everyone wonder whether the Cup races would take place at all. The NYYC decided that there was dirty work at the cross roads and that perhaps, after all, Ben Lexcen was not the genius who designed the winged keel, but some Dutch scientist where he had tested *Australia II*'s design.

One or two Dutchmen who had been involved when Lexcen, with NYYC permission, had used the facilities at Wageningen, claimed that they were the designers of the keel and not he. When the NYYC sent emissaries to try to make them sign affidavits to that end, no one would put pen to paper. There was almost open warfare between the Americans and the Australians and it was prolonged until the very last minute. We waited, wondering whether the NYYC would have the nerve to call off the racing. It was a close run thing, but then so too was the racing when it did get underway.

The scenario was such that had a screenwriter offered it to a film producer, he would have had it rejected for being too much of a 'Boy's Own Paper' story. The Cup races had almost everything and there is no doubt that the right boat won, but she should never have taken that long.

121

Liberty was two up due to gear failures on *Australia II* after the first two races. The failures were uncharacteristic for an Australian boat, but they were failures which cost dearly. The third race went according to plan for the Aussies and the writing should have been on Dennis Conner's wall in bright green and gold letters but he refused to see them. The fourth race of the 1983 *America*'s Cup saw Dennis Conner produce the most tactically brilliant sailing to put the American's 3-1 up. It was, agreed everyone, an impregnable position. Perhaps someone should have told Bertrand, Hugh Treharne and the Aussie crew.

Then *Liberty* had her share of bad luck when an hydraulic ram on one of her jumper struts gave way. Two men, Tom Rich and Scott Vogel, spent the best part of an hour up the mast, clearing the old one away and fitting a new one rushed out by speedboat, finishing their job after the ten minute gun had fired. It was hardly a settled state for Conner and his crew from which to expect to win. They didn't. The replacement ram gave way and that must have hampered *Liberty* even though the wind was as brisk as it had been all summer and the depowering of the mainsail on one tack was not as speed reducing as it would have been in a lighter breeze.

Conner had claimed that when the breeze died earlier in the series with *Australia II* ahead and the time limit ran out before she could finish, that God was an American. God changed sides soon after the start of the sixth race and gave *Australia II* a lift which took her from being astern and to windward to ahead and to windward and a lead of two and a half minutes at the weather mark. Not even Dennis Conner can expect to come back from that in a 12-Metre match race. The score was 3-3 and those of us reporting the event could scarce believe our luck.

We had a story that was leaping out of the sports pages on to the front pages around the world. For the freelancers, it meant a highly gratuitous pay day was ahead. Stan Zemanek, for whose Australian radio network I was contributing during the races, and I both worked late in the Armory before crossing Thames Street to The Ark for dinner. We were joined by Stan's wife, Marcella, and daughter, Gaby. Confrey Phillips was tinkling the keyboard of the piano in the upstairs restaurant; the tune was 'My Little Room in Bloomsbury,' as we walked in. There are some trivia one always remembers. We sat down, not only to eat, but also to discuss how we would handle our coverage of the big event; the showdown at Newport.

Never before had there been a seventh race and Alan Bond had decided that we should wait, calling for a lay day to allow the nerves of *Australia II*'s crew to settle.

The next scheduled day dawned with very little wind and the race committee called that one off. It was time for Dennis Conner to get in on the act and he requested a lay day for Sunday 25 September, left his crew to play with the boat's ballast and hived off to play golf.

The ballast stayed right where it was, with *Liberty* in her light air mode and the choice was correct. There was not a lot of wind and the start was delayed an hour. On board the *New Englander II* (the *Hel-Cat* had finally lost the job as press boat), Stan and I had been talking with only breaks for the commercials from a quarter of an hour before the race should have been under way. No one was happier than when it did in a light southerly. *Australia II* led in the early stages and then *Liberty* made use of a header. She tacked, cleared *Australia II*'s bows and rounded the weather mark with a twenty-nine second lead.

The little Aussie battlers pulled back just six seconds on the two reaches but on the next leg, Dennis Conner sailed as well as he is ever likely to. He was sensationally brilliant. He went where he wanted to go and forced Bertrand to go where it was far from beneficial. The result was that *Liberty* led by 57 seconds at the weather mark. There were those who had gone below and were writing their final story, a tale of the Aussies who had come so close and been battered into submission by the might of the world's greatest technological nation at the last.

I could not do that. Radio 2UE and its affiliates across Australia was hanging on our words and, as Stan had told them more than once in the series, 'its not over 'til the fat lady sings.' We had to stay to the death. Out on the racecourse, Dennis Conner was uneasy. He believed that he had to have at least one and a quarter minutes lead to be safe on the run and when a windshift came his way, he gybed and went down the best angle to the mark.

Behind him, Hugh Treharne had seen a darkening of the water out on the other flank of the course – it meant more wind beyond where the line of spectator craft were parked. Hugh informed John Bertrand and they stayed on their tack. And it was that which swung the match. The boats split widely; Conner playing the angles while Bertrand went for more wind, never mind where it was coming from. We held our breath. Some time soon they had to gybe and converge. Then, and only then, would we know the truth. Even Stan had given up speculating, he had gone for an Australian return in 1986 and that was what he was telling our listeners. He called me to confirm it, but I had seen the change of angles and took the microphone to refute it. I hung on to that mike for two minutes as the boats converged, determined to be the one to tell a large proportion of Australia that their boat was back in with a sporting chance. More than that, she led shortly after and at the leeward mark the margin was twenty-one seconds in her favour.

Stan was up and running at full speed too and what a story we had to tell. Both boats tacked forty-seven times on that final beat, Bertrand was not going to allow Conner out of his wind shadow. On this the future of the *America*'s Cup was to be decided and Bertrand was in no mood for mistakes.

Forty-one seconds it was at the finish; forty-one seconds that changed the face of yachting history. The scenes which followed were those of disbelief, of joy, of relief and of despair. The difficult thing, quite often, was to judge who was displaying which and why. Conner, on the edge of losing emotional control (and who would have blamed him if he had), faced the press and said, after congratulating Alan Bond, 'Today, *Australia II* was just a better boat. And they beat us.'

He cleared the stage for the Australians, led by the man who had been the Svengali all summer long, Warren Jones. To him much of the credit for this win was due. He introduced each of the crew in turn and then likened the summer to a game of chess and then, using an Australianism and a gesture to go with it, said that on this day it was 'Mate'.

There was weeping and wailing in the streets and there was carousing in the bars. For us, however, there was none of that. Stories had to be filed around the world and it was well after midnight before I emerged from the Armory.

Detritus littered the streets but the bars were shut and the folks gone home. I knew one place where there would still be a welcome. There was a house, rented for the summer by Rupert Murdoch's media men, known to its denizens as the Royal Heartbreak Hotel. There, I was sure there would still be a cold beer and someone to talk to. I wasn't wrong. The first one didn't hit the sides and I took the next one to a table and sat down on a dining chair.

The next thing I knew was my shoulder being shook and Bob Ross saying that it was half past four and time to go home. The second can was hardly touched.

The next morning as I walked from the house where I was staying, I met Warren Jones walking down the road to collect his bicycle from the boatyard where it had been abandoned. He wore a puzzled frown and I asked him the cause. 'I just can't think where in Fremantle we are going to hold the *America*'s Cup Ball!'

One set of worries were over and another set beginning. I thought more of Newport and its future. It had been home to me for more than two years, on and off, now my returns would be few. I was sad. I think that was obvious from one of the pieces I wrote that morning for the *Guardian* – A requiem for Newport.

"Newport, Rhode Island is fiercely proud of its heritage. Like the New Englanders themselves, Newport is steeped in early colonial history and it was, until yesterday, the home of *America*'s Cup races. Huge billboards on the side of the highways proclaim that fact as you enter Rhode Island – 'the greatest little state in the union' – the 'Ocean State.' Now they will have to go and Newport is bereft of its jewel.

Despite the parties, Newport itself was stilled in the early hours. The clapboard houses even seemed to have withdrawn. In Pelham Street, the first in America to be lit by gas – by David Melville in 1805 – to the intersection; along Spring Street past the spotlit white wooden spire of Trinity Church to the imposing pillared facade of the Littlefield-Van Zandt house. In the tiny cemetery next door a grey squirrel busied himself burying hazelnuts blissfully unaware that a few hours earlier Newport real estate values had taken a severe knock.

Without the Cup many of the large houses will never again find a full summer's rent – between them the 10 syndicates this summer rented more that 20 of varying sizes. I walked past the Capitol Realty Company, to whom I had given money in 1974 for an

125

apartment while Alan Bond, Ben Lexcen and John Bertrand – this year's triumphal trio from Western Australia – put together their first effort with a boat called *Southern Cross*, a bright yellow 12-metre known familiarly as 'The Custard Bucket'. The Realty Company will not see my pennies again and those of a good many higher rollers besides.

What too of the bars, bistros and boutiques which since the US fleet left here in the 1970s have sprung up on the wharves? Can Newport without the Cup support their vast numbers? The tourists will not have the attraction of the 12-metre sailors who are reputed, by their presence in Newport for the racing, to help swell the annual turnover in Rhode Island state by $300 million. The Candy Store and the Black Pearl are institutions on Bannister's Wharf that will never perish. When Ted Turner won the Cup in 1977 his crew were awarded gold cards – free drinks for life – at the Candy Store. Now perhaps they would be better off with similar facilities at the Tum Tum Tree in Fremantle.

Newport will sleep uneasily this winter. No longer is it a dream world.

'Requiem for a racing town' *by Bob Fisher –*
The Guardian, 28 September 1983.

Chapter Seven

Brightlingsea – a remarkable little town

Cruising guides, written by those who have gone before, often inspire confidence. By their very being, they point to the writer's success and the possibly hazardous passage becomes a veritable breeze. How did the navigators of an earlier age proceed without them; imagine the first men to find the entrance to what is now Sydney Harbour and how they would have possibly pursued a passage. Or, more simply, the first amateur sailors who wished to navigate around the East Coast of England; theirs was an adventure, even if, for the professionals, there were aids to navigation. Just a hundred years ago, Frank Cowper began his series of five books, *Sailing Tours*, the first of them was centred on his cruising around the coasts of Essex and Suffolk, so that amateur sailors would benefit from his practical experience with a series of books. He found that 'our only guide was a chart,' and these were unreliable. One, purported to 'be corrected to 1891' (he wrote the following year) had a lighthouse shown coloured red, 'as if it still existed, although, as a matter of fact, it had ceased to exist for at least thirty years.' I found his narrative, as he left the Blackwater and headed for the Colne, singularly poignant. True, the detail is altered now, but there is still much in his description that would fit today.

"In spite of the jeers of the others they were obliged to confess that they did not know half as much about Layer Marney as we did. They had rowed up as far as Virley, and being tired had bought photographs of the Towers and tried to talk as if they knew all about it. This day may count as one of our boat expeditions ashore, and none the less interesting on that account. Next morning we started with the first of the ebb, and with a breeze east by south it was a dead beat down to the red and white Bench Head buoy. By the way, these buoys are not very easy to distinguish, as regards colour at any rate. The North Buxey buoy is especially poor in this respect, and a small buoy into the bargain.

Instead of going down the regular channel it is possible to go to the north of the Bench Head in 6ft of water in lowest springs, but the passage is very narrow, and has a sharp turn just south of the white Fishery buoy on the west side of the Colne; it is better, therefore, to run no risks, seeing we are strangers, and to keep to the proper channel.

As the wind is dead ahead, and the tide is setting out strong, we must be careful not to reach overmuch inside of the line we already indicated, viz., the North-West Knowl buoy (red and white striped), in line with the Red Eagle buoy, until we are abreast of the Bench Head buoy, when we can go to the southward of this line, but only to within a cable's length of the west of the North-West Knowl, for the bank takes a turn to the northward here, and shoals to 12ft close to the buoy.

From a distance all the buoys are deceptive, and as it is quite easy to get aground anywhere about this patchy entrance to the Colne and Blackwater, great care must be taken not to confuse the buoys. The Knowl buoy is a really fine fellow, and has a kind of apron on him, on which his name is painted; there is no mistaking this mark. The Bar buoy is also a conspicuous one, with it's staff and globe on the top. When once these two are made out the rest follow naturally. In hazy weather the shore is decidedly vague all round here; in fact, from the Knowl buoy it is difficult to see any leading marks if there is much haze about. The buoys are the best guides.

It took us about an hour to beat down from our anchorage in Mersea quarters to the North-West Knowl, but now we have a fine breeze up the Colne.

After leaving the red buoy on our starboard our chart marks only one more buoy on either side. As a matter of fact there are at least two on the starboard in addition to the one already marked, and three on the port. The channel narrows very fast, until off Mersea Point it is barely a quarter of a mile wide at low water, but it widens out a little more afterwards where the Pyefleet joins the Colne.

The entrance to the river is rather pretty, with Mersea Island on the port, and the hill, with the Martello tower on the top, on the starboard.

We have a choice of creeks to explore when once we are inside the Colne. Brightlingsea lies on our right and the Pyefleet on our left. Ahead of us stretches the Colne, with the young flood bearing us up towards Colchester.

We have now come to a business centre of the yachting interests, where the inhabitants are all more or less dependent on this luxurious pastime. There are always many yachts lying up at Brightlingsea Creek, and many more about six miles farther up the Colne at Wivenhoe and Rowhedge, otherwise called East Donyland.

Abreast of the Mersea Point there are also usually several large steam and sailing yachts at anchor. One fine steam yacht of about 700 tons was pointed out to us, which had been at her moorings over three years. She belonged to an American we were told. (The yacht was the *Valfreya*, owned by Mr Bayard Brown who kept her with steam up in readiness for a cruise around the world which never materialised.) There seems a want of progress about this gentleman not usual in his countrymen. Pretty as we found the entrance to the Colne, we fancy we should feel it a little monotonous if we had to lie there for three years at anchor in a vessel perfectly found in every respect and well suited to cruise around the world.

As the tide is fair to carry us up to Wivenhoe, and will also do to bring us back again, we decide to stand up the Colne as far as we can with comfort, and then put about and anchor off Brightlingsea for the night.

The channel is marked with a buoy or two here and there, but they are not very conspicuous. However, until about a mile past Alresford Creek on our right, over which the branch line from Colchester to Brightlingsea passes, the channel is easy, lying for the most part in mid-stream.

After passing Alresford Creek keep to the starboard side until we can see right down to Wivenhoe, when bear over to the left, and keep so for half a mile. Then steer in mid-stream straight for Wivenhoe. The land is rather high on the right, and the wind, being north-east comes in puffs. This is the more bothering, as the channel is very narrow, and there are a good many craft about. Wivenhoe is a kind of Essex Haslar Creek, and is wholly devoted to yachts. Certainly it is a very handy place, and there is no other creek so suitable for its easy access to London as this Colne River. The Crouch might very easily compete with it; indeed, to our minds it is far preferable, and is destined in the future, now that the Great Eastern have opened it up so effectually by their new line, to become the handiest place for Londoners. At present it takes the same time to get to Wivenhoe, although the distance is considerably greater, as it does to get to Burnham; but once the Crouch gets known it is certain to go rapidly ahead. Its advantages are so much greater in every way. It is nearer town, has deeper water, is a finer creek, and is much easier to get into. It is Colchester which has made the Colne more important. But for pleasant easy sailing, we have no tidal waters near London which can offer such attractions as the Crouch.

There is nothing to induce us to stay at Wivenhoe. We might sail up to the Hythe at Colchester if we like, but there is little gained by it, and the channel is narrow and shallow. Colchester is a fine old town, but we can visit it more conveniently by taking the train from Brightlingsea. So down with the helm and let her come round. It is a soldier's wind back again fortunately, for if we had to beat down the creek we should find it tedious work.

The view down the river is prettier than it was coming up. The country is hilly on each side, and here and there old farmhouses peep out from their sheltering copses hard by.

As we pass Langenhoe Creek we see Peldon church tower some two miles inland. This church suffered greatly from the earthquake which did such damage to Layer Marney Towers.

In entering Brightlingsea Creek from the Colne we must be careful not to get aground on the spit which stretches out some way from the north-east shore. The creek itself is very shallow, and if we go far in we shall ground on the mud.

If we can find room, the best place to bring up is off the hard, which here is a kind of low wooden causeway, reaching down nearly to low-water mark.

There is nothing to see in Brightlingsea itself, but if we have energy enough we ought to visit St. Osyth Priory. It is possible to row up to within a quarter of a mile of it, but the more certain way is to land on the east shore, and walk up. The house is interesting, although at the dissolution of a the monasteries the greater part of the monastic buildings were pulled down. The estates were granted to Lord Cromwell, but very soon after reverted to the Crown.**"**

From 'Sailing Tours' *By Frank Cowper*

What staggers me is that the usually observant Cowper has missed the singularly most important landmark for anyone heading from the Bench Head buoy up the Colne – Bateman's Tower. This strange edifice of three storeys is everyone's guide to a proper passage up the Colne and was certainly there when Cowper went from Virley Creek to the Colne. It was built, as a bathing house by Squire John Bateman in 1882, some nine years prior to Cowper's cruise, and has withstood the weathering of more than a century and the threats of the local council to pull it down.

During World War II, it was used by the local branch of the Royal Observer Corps and subsequently was the Colne Yacht Club's starting platform. Many's the race which I have started from there and the same gentleman that started those races was responsible for me having my Sunday breakfast there with him during the war years – my father.

It was the ROC which removed the elegant conical roof from the tower in order that they might more easily spot the aircraft. It was a pity that part of the war reparations didn't insist on the Corps replacing it so that today it would look exactly as Cowper would have seen it.

Sitting at Splash Point, at the entrance to Brightlingsea Creek, and looking at Bateman's Tower on 22 January 1981, inspired me to pen the following lines.

The Spring tide lifts the flotsam
High into the foreshore's samphire;
The calm sea rises and falls
As a body breathing,
While over all
The sea-mist hangs.

Beyond the watch-tower on the point
There is but greyness;
Maybe the outline of the further shore
Tantalises as an hallucination,
Like a desert oasis
While the sea-mist hangs.

There is an eerie stillness
Of shadows and reflections
Cast on the mirrored water
For which there is no horizon,
As olive green and olive grey
Of sea and sea-mist blend.

The dripping damp suppresses life
Only the gulls maintain their round;
The skylarks' shrill cries are
Soon lost in the misty blanket,
Even the stolid fisherman capitulates
To wend home catchless.

The sea's weed and it's regurgitations
Are left behind to stifle

The fringe of samphire on the muddy shore.
Gone are the birds as stillness
Coalesces with the early darkness
To coagulate the sea-mist.

The 22nd January 1981 by Bob Fisher

Those who are born by the waterside have a distinct advantage in following a career or pastime as a sailor over those who are brought up 'in the air of dark-roomed town'. Some are lucky enough to have begun life steeped in a heritage of the sea, in a village where the majority of the men earned their living directly from boats of one form or another. The choice wasn't mine, but there are few places I would, in retrospect, have been happier with than Brightlingsea, however scathingly Cowper may have been that there was nothing to see. I did have the advantage of using that 'low wooden causeway', indeed it was the centre of my life during the formative years and I am happy that it is still there in an adequate state of repair.

Some of my earliest memories are the tales I heard from the veteran mariners who sat in the shelter at the top of the Hard, gnarled men whose life had been a constant battle with the elements and yet who could not bear to be away from the sea, even in the very twilight of their lives. They came from generations who had known the hardships of fishing in the winter and yachting in the summer. Some had been at the soft edge of the trade, the stewards and the cooks, but even their calling didn't totally protect them from the dangers as I used to be reminded on 6 June each year by George Savory, our milkman and a former yacht hand. He would tell us that it was this or that many years ago that George Lewes had been lost off *Astra* when she was racing off Southend.

The incident was reported in *The Yachtsman* of 8 June 1935.

"Racing on Thursday at Southend, in which England's big yachts were engaged, had a tragic sequel. Mr George Lewes, a steward, of Brightlingsea, fell overboard from Mr Hugh Paul's *Astra* and was drowned. It was very rough weather, and Mr Sopwith's

133

famous *Endeavour* had to be towed to the Medway with broken masts and sails awash.

Both accidents happened about the same time, when the yachts were on the second leg of the course, from the West Oaze to the Mouse Lightship. First, *Astra*'s crew accidentally let go of the spinnaker sheet while trying to get it in, and the sail blew out like a kite. In trying to get it in Lewes fell overboard. Captain Heard did everything possible to save him. *Astra*'s boat was smartly launched, with two men in it and two lifebuoys, promptly thrown, fell near Lewes who was swimming. *Velsheda*, which was following, tacked in the hope of giving assistance. But *Astra* was running before the wind, sheets free, at eleven knots, and by the time the boat had reached the spot where Lewes had been swimming he had disappeared.

Up to a late hour on Thursday the body had not been recovered. Mr Paul was greatly upset by the tragedy. *Yankee* and *Velsheda* were the only yachts to finish the race, *Yankee* winning."

George Lewes was 51, married with two sons and a daughter. He was the son of an old yacht captain and was an experienced hand. He is commemorated by the 191st tile in a frieze that runs around the inside of Brightlingsea's parish church, All Saints', a frieze which was the idea of the Vicar, Canon Arthur Pertwee, after the disaster of 6 March 1883 in which the lives of nineteen men of the parish were lost at sea.

Len Southern, who was the local papers' reporter and 'stringer' for a number of the nationals, related the disaster in his *Stories of the Colne*.

"The month of March, 1883, will ever be sadly memorable in Brightlingsea. It will be to a seafaring people the anniversary of the most ill-fated voyage that was ever made from this port, and will bring back in many a home, that memory of a husband, a father or a brother who will return no more. It will remind the whole community of a grievous and irreparable loss of life in the dark, cold waters of the North Sea.

It was about the 1st of March that a fleet of 15 of our vessels, carrying six hands each, set sail for the Terschelling oyster-grounds in the North Sea. Wind and weather were fair, and the good success of the last trip on the same quest had given the expedition a more than usually hopeful departure.

The destination of the vessels was quickly reached, then three days of calm succeeded. Then on Monday night, 5 March, a light breeze, which had been blowing during the day from the north, suddenly became a furious gale.

Almost as much of this could be guessed at home, and on Tuesday and Wednesday, the fierce gusts of wind and blinding snowstorms turned everybody's thoughts to the same direction. And many were the anxious remarks exchanged respecting the fortunes of the 'Skilling Fleet.'

The full force of the gale however, was scarcely felt at home, and it was confidently hoped that the boats would safely weather the storm, as they had weathered others, apparently worse, before.

The sight, however, presented by two of the vessels which returned on Thursday morning, the *Express* and the *Glance*, both in battered condition, the former with her flag half-masted, filled all hearts with dismay and alarm. The signal of mourning displayed by the *Express* noted the loss of one of her crew, who had been washed off the deck by a tremendous sea that boarded her about seven o'clock on Tuesday morning.

More and more anxiously now was awaited the appearance of the remainder of the fleet. Thursday night and Friday morning brought home the *Vandura*, the *Dream* and the *Care*, and the last to arrive was the *Heiress* on Friday morning.

But what had become of the *Recruit* and the *Conquest* and the Yarmouth lugger *Mascotte*? More or less hopeful answers were found for such questions, but the men who knew the North Sea best were, for the most part, grave and silent. Saturday dawned and closed a blank. Then came Sunday, a day of fearful suspense that will not soon be forgotten in Brightlingsea. Prayers were offered at all services in church for those in sorrow or anxiety at home, and for those who might be still in peril on the sea.

Next day, the condition of public feeling was evidence by the numbers of people gathered on the Hard, standing in groups, or

135

pacing an imaginary deck's length, in spite of the cutting snow squalls. Some mounted the various accessible elevations, telescope in hand, to take a survey of the offing for the hundredth time, while a hollow attempt would now and then be made to relieve the tension by watching the children at play with snowballs.

A painful incident occurred that morning. Two vessels heaving in sight were at once pronounced to be two of the three missing boats so eagerly looked for. The joyous news spread like wildfire through the town, only to be followed immediately afterwards by a cruel and bitter contradiction. The vessels sighted were not the *Recruit* or the *Conquest* or the *Mascotte*.

This was almost the last flicker of hope 'ere the darkness of despair closed in, and the families of the missing men drew down their blinds, and acknowledged the sad reality of their losses.

A melancholy sight the whole town soon presented, with signs of mourning on every side, from the flag half-masted on the church tower to the darkened windows in the cottages.

Of the three ill-fated vessels there is nothing more to tell. Not the least traces of them have since been discovered, and probably their fate will ever remain a mystery. Nineteen men perished in the disaster, involving nineteen families, and thirty two children were fatherless."

From 'Stories of the Colne' *by L.W.Southern*

Len was certainly one of the 'fire and brimstone' school of writers but that loss of its men was to the tiny fishing village of 1883 what a pit disaster was to the villages in the mining areas of the country would have been. It was enough to stimulate the Reverend Arthur Pertwee to work back in the records to his induction in 1872, to find what other lives had been lost at sea in that time. He found 39 others before the awful tragedy of 6 March 1883 and with the help of Churchwarden William Stammers, who gave £200 to the project as well as considerable time and effort, he started the frieze of memorial tiles.

Since that time there have been a total of 212 erected and there are but a few spaces left – in 1983, when it was suggested at a Parish meeting that

136

it would appropriate to complete the frieze that year, a relative of mine demurred on the grounds that he was one of the last professional seamen living in the town! – they record the diversity of livings which the Brightlingsea men sought in peace as in war.

There is a tile for a seaman on the *Titanic* (another Brightlingsea man survived), another for one lost from HMS *Queen Mary* at the Battle of Jutland, one man lost when his ship was sunk by a submarine in the first world war and another who was lost in a submarine in the second. There are only seven since 1945, one of them for Alfred Richard Pawle, my uncle, who was lost when the yacht *Wanderling*, which he was delivering, sank in The Wash on 15 December 1950.

In my early childhood, I was given two unbreakable rules. I must never make the mainsheet fast, nor might I stand up in a dinghy. The tiles bear witness to a man who broke one of those rules, Albert Barber, who was drowned in the Harbour on Easter Day 1953, aged 76. He stood up in a dinghy, when ferrying a party to their yacht, as he came alongside their boat was tipped out. The Parish Magazine recorded 54 years earlier how another man had lost his life by breaking the other golden rule. Fred Richardson, his wife and her sister, had borrowed a small sailing boat and was struck by a squall which capsized her. All three were drowned and when the boat was found and righted, it was discovered that 'the sheet of the sail had been made fast to a thwart, to which, in a sudden squall, may be attributed the cause of the accident'.

Others from the parish have been more fortunate and lived to tell their tales of derring-do. One such was Charles Barnes who was the only one left aboard a fishing smack in the English Channel when his five companions were washed overboard. Most of the boat's gear, together with her hatches, were washed away and Barnes had first to nail some of her sails over the hatches to prevent the smack from filling before he could sail her to port. He made it into Shoreham and was rewarded with an inscribed silver watch by the Brightlingsea Smack Club, the local co-operative insurance society.

Men of this parish were among those who went on strike in 1934 from the *America*'s Cup challenger, *Endeavour*. Much malignment has fallen on them in the intervening years and all because the wrong interpretation of their action had been universally placed. They didn't strike for higher wages, inspired by the knowledge of what their American counterparts were to receive, but for the loss in wages they would suffer because the racing went on into September when they would otherwise have been engaged in fishing.

At the end of the season, the last week in August, these men would have been laid off from their yachting job with a week's pay and their racing bonus; immediately, they would have had to have found a job on a fishing smack working out of their home port. Because *Endeavour*'s crew would have been in America when the fishing boats' crews were made up, they would have had no job all winter long. What they sought from Sir T.O.M. Sopwith was the money to cover that which they would have lost fishing. Nearly fifty years later, when I interviewed Sir T.O.M. Sopwith for Southern Television, he admitted that not granting their request was one of the mistakes he had made in life, but, he added, the men had not made their problem clear or he might have taken a different view then.

They were hard days indeed but they were almost forever wiped away by an act of the fishermen themselves who in the late nineteen forties and early fifties went in search of a white weed that grew in the Thames Estuary. They sold it for decorative and crude pharmaceutical purposes, but in scraping it into their trawls, they destroyed the ecology that supported the food cycle which had the fish at a prime point. Their greed for the weed proved to be the undoing of the fishing industry in the area and at one time there was only one working smack out of Brightlingsea and that skippered by the man with the most unlikely name, Basil Steady – the name unlikely because of his less than temperate habits ashore. At sea, and that I can vouch for personally, Basil was a sober seaman and a fisherman who had that strange sense of knowing just where the fish would run. Ashore, Basil was a different man but he always had a smile on his face.

The mariners of Brightlingsea in the later years became those whose exploits could be found written on the pages of the yachting magazines. Much of that centres around Reg White, who, had he been born thirty years later would have been the first millionaire professional sailor. As it was, he achieved fame for winning the Little America's Cup on no less than four occasions, was twice Yachtsman of the Year and gained the first Olympic gold medal awarded for catamaran racing in 1976 and contested the trials for another twelve years before finally admitting that he had handed over the role of the country's best two-hulled sailor to his son, Robert.

138

When Reg and I wrote our book, *Catamaran Racing*, back in 1968, Reg recorded the time when the C-Class, in which the Little America's Cup is raced, where Britain had always held an edge, was rocked by the appearance of new technology from the Antipodes in the form of a wing-mast on *Quest II*. Reg was very circumspect in his report of the series which he sailed with *Emma Hamilton*, a two-year-old Rod Macalpine-Downie design built by his own firm.

"When the day of the first race came the forecast was for strongish breezes and we decided to use the lower aspect ratio mainsail on *Emma*. What a mistake that turned out to be. The expected wind didn't materialise and *Quest II* beat us home. This was the first time I had ever been behind in the series and I didn't like it. Up went the tall sail and there it stayed for the rest of the match. We won the next three races in medium to strongish breezes and everyone thought that it was all over bar the shouting, but I was far from happy. *Quest II* was obviously faster than *Emma* in all conditions and I was only able to hold her off by intense tactical sailing. It was important to get the best start, throw all the dirty wind I could at her on the beats, and fight tooth and nail downwind. The Australians were getting better in every race; they hadn't the advantages I had enjoyed in close combat racing in the trials, but they were learning fast. They took the next two races. All square and one race to go, and what a race that turned out to be.

Quest II took an early lead. She was now beating faster than *Emma* and we were catching up downwind. The tuning of both teams had reversed the original roles. We were just not able to get ahead but were very close at the end of the downwind legs. It was blowing pretty hard throughout the race and there were some pretty hefty gusts streaking across the Thames Estuary. On the penultimate leg, a run, we were rapidly closing on *Quest II* when a really vicious squall caught both of us and *Quest II* capsized. I've since had time to analyse the reason for her capsize. Because of the strength of the wind and to get the best advantage from it we were tacking downwind. In the lighter patches you luff to keep the boat travelling fast and then bear away in the gusts. At the time of the

139

capsize *Quest II* was about four boat lengths ahead of us and about a hundred yards to windward. The direct line to the buoy was about a hundred yards further to leeward. *Quest II* was running off towards the mark before the squall hit her and she had nothing left in hand to ease. When she caught the full effect of the elements she buried her bow and cartwheeled. In *Emma Hamilton*, we were broad reaching as the squall struck and were able to bear away and ease the pressure somewhat by keeping the apparent wind in the same position. Lady Luck may have smiled on us but I am sure that seamanship saved the day. John and I took it very quietly up the final beat to the finish and I don't think I've ever been more relieved to hear a finishing gun. The slower boat had successfully defended the trophy, but the C-Class in Britain had received a very nasty shock.**"**

From 'Catamaran Racing' *by Reg White & Bob Fisher*

There were so many shades of the slightly senior event, the *America*'s Cup, about that – slower boats winning, Australia coming from behind to level the series – which meant technology in the little East Coast town had to redress the balance before the next challenge a year later. It produced the wing-masted *Lady Helmsman* which successfully defended the Cup on three subsequent occasions.

The efficacy of the *Lady Helmsman* campaign was, in great part, due to the highly commercial sponsorship it received from Helmsman Paints. It was the forerunner of other campaigns in the C-Class, notably from cigarette manufacturers, and it upped the pace of development of racing catamarans in much the same way that the French have been able to do with their offshore multihulls because the publicity which they have generated has encouraged sponsors.

This did, however, have a downside which became dreadfully obvious when the first rush of sponsorship dried up. The fact that as a result of the publicity which *Lady Helmsman* generated, the paint company captured a 28 per cent share of the yacht paint market from an almost stationary start, cut very little ice. With the source of money gone, the development stopped and the year after *Lady Helmsman*'s three successful defences of the Cup, Reg was forced to defend with an even older pair of hulls and one of the spare rigs from the previous year's campaign. It was hardly surprising therefore that the domination of Britain in the C-Class came to an end. The Little America's Cup went to Denmark for a brief sojourn and then became the province of the United States and Australia. To retrieve it will need substantial funds as the Americans and Australians have moved the game into a new field.

Brightlingsea still produces the world's fastest racing catamarans and as long as Reg White continues to build them, it will need something of a revolution to take away that crown. One only wonders how the fishermen/yacht hands of yester-year would have thought about Brightlingsea's present place in yacht racing.

Chapter Eight

Fourteens Are Forever

The stories of Uffa Fox are boundless – the man truly was a legend in his own lifetime. He lived life to the full and probably gave the sport of sailing more than any other human being. His sense of humour and his hell-raising went hand in hand – what other person would have dared to put a whoopee cushion on the dining chair of a reigning Queen – not too many people have the monarch to dinner in the first place. Uffa was loved by all but his creditors and most of them forgave him the wait, although the monarch took a long time before she set foot on the Isle of Wight again.

His dinner parties were substantial affairs; the port and the Stilton lingered long after the roasts and puddings had been consumed, and with them came the conversation and the singing. Uffa was never one to let fall an invitation nor an opportunity to sing. A scant percentage would have been publicly acceptable but he did record some songs of the sea and to listen to them brings memories of the old rogue.

My most precious is of a visit to his house on the Cowes waterfront on the first Sunday evening of Cowes Week 1971. I went with a BBC Radio crew to record the comments of the great man for the 'Today' programme about the local lad he had chosen to crew Prince Charles in a Flying Fifteen for the week. Uffa emerged, black tie and collar awry, from one of his noisy

142

dinner parties and asked us to return an hour later. This we duly did. The opportunity seemed to me ripe to ask him a few extra questions and I did. He was just ripe for the interview and my five questions and his five answers made a daily insert into 'Today' throughout the Week.

Uffa was far ahead of his time in yacht design. His much used phrase, 'weight has value only in a steam-roller', showed his love for light displacement; he thought that all yachts should be little more than scaled-up dinghies. His dinghies and their derivatives still continue to give great pleasure. His *Avenger*, International 14 K135, was the first planing dinghy designed so to do and from her a complete breed of boats evolved. Many are raced today and there are several who served in the 1939-45 war who were grateful to Uffa for his airborne lifeboat design, many of which he bought and destroyed after the war so that there wouldn't be too many who had a 'cheap' Uffa Fox yacht.

He was a multi-facetted man who gave freely of his knowledge as was exhibited in the letters he wrote to Michael Bratby to enable him to sail the International 14 which he had designed and built for him to greater advantage. He began at the beginning.

**"To Michael Bratby Esq
Canoe *Brynhild*,
Isle de Brehat

My dear Michael,
You have asked me to write a series of letters on how to sail your International 14-footer *Whisper*, and I write the first inside the tent of my canoe in this dear little harbour on the Brittany coast, where we are at present cruising, and having a great deal of pleasure.

It is rather difficult to know just which part of sailing to describe first, but since in sailing all your power is from the winds of Heaven, I will try and describe them first, as without wind you cannot sail, and it is only by a thorough study of winds that one reaches perfection in sailing. This first letter, therefore, is of the wind, which drives the sailing vessel.

143

Westerly Winds

Now, as you know, the winds blow from all points of the compass, and they are affected by the shape and contour of the land. First of all I will try and tell you what I know of the south-west, our prevailing wind. This wind comes in from the Atlantic laden with moisture and so brings rain with it, which means that throughout our summer we get wet days, as the south-west is our summer wind and August brings the height of the south-west monsoon, when generally the winds are strong and rain frequent.

When you are sailing with a south-west wind, watch for the heavier clouds, for not only do they generally bring heavier winds or squalls with them, but they are often inclined to shift the wind a point or so, and if you are headed on one tack a point, by going about you will be freed a point on the other and so pick up several places. For this reason every small boat should carry a compass, which will immediately indicate any shift of wind, these little dinghies of course making a right angle to their old tack when beating to windward.

In fairly good weather this south-west wind is very light through the early morning and does not reach its strength until towards midday (we have put the clocks on one hour through the summer months). All through the afternoon it blows quite hard, and towards five in the evening it starts to ease away again, and generally by 8 o'clock it is almost calm again. That is your true day's breeze; it comes with the day, increasing towards noon and decreasing in the evening. Then when the night comes the wind will draw offshore, say north-west instead of south-west, the cause of this being that in fine weather the sun heats the land, causing the air to rise over it, which is replaced by air sucked in from the sea; the hotter the day the stronger the wind. Then, too, at night the land cools off quickly, the sea remaining at much the same temperature, and so at night the sea is warmer than the land and draws the wind off the shore.

Easterly Winds

North and easterly winds are never true in strength or direction. All over the North Atlantic, even down in the steady north-east Trades,

144

there are heavy squalls, which sometimes shift as much as four points and so always when racing with an easterly wind keep a look-out for a shift of wind, and also for variation in strength. These are dry winds, and we seldom get rain with them, but they are not met with very much between Whitsun and the end of August; in September and up to Easter they frequently blow for many days on end, but of course at that time of year little racing is indulged in.

As can easily be understood, wind speeds of various strengths exert various pressures or capsizing moments on a sailing vessel. Most racers think about reefing when it is blowing about 20 miles an hour, though they often carry full sail when it is blowing 5 miles an hour harder than that. The reefing depends a great deal upon the condition of the sea, for if a sea is rough and does not suit the boat she is often out of water for half her length, which means as far as power is concerned that she has only half the stability in her hull, so it is difficult to lay down any hard and fast rule for reefing, and therefore the following is only an indication of what to do.

Wind speeds and pressures:

Speed in mph	Pressure in Lbs/sq ft
0	.0
2	.01
5	.08
9	.28
14	.67
19	1.31
24	2.3
30	3.6
37	5.4
44	7.7
52	10.5
60	14.0

You will see by this table of wind speeds and pressures, taken from Brown's Nautical Almanac, that from 19 miles an hour to 30 miles per hour, the pressure has increased on the sails practically three times, so as 20 miles an hour is the reefing point, at 30 miles an hour you must carry less than half of your total sail area.

It is well to remember that in racing you reef so that you are comfortable during the lulls, but when cruising you reef still more so that you are comfortable during the hard squalls. In a 14-footer you can ease your mainsheet in the twinkling of an eye, so that though normally you would be overpowered and capsizing in the heavy squalls, by easing your mainsheet in these, and letting the jib pull her through, you are fairly comfortable.

This playing of the mainsheet is much like playing a heavy fish on a light line; the line will break, we will say, at a 300 lb pull, and yet your fish weighs 900 lbs and can put that weight on the line, so that all the time you are playing this fish you have to be alert and sensitive to his every move, and see that you never get more than 280 lbs on the line, hauling him in and letting him go, a process calling for the greatest skill; and if you think that with your mainsheet you have the same problem, and can excel in this art, you will soon win races in hard squally weather just as I did with *Avenger*, as it is this alone that has enabled 14-footers to race in places like Lowestoft when the 12-metres dare not risk their masts in the wind and sea running.

The wind is invisible, and though they say pigs can see it, we cannot, and so we have to judge its speeds by the angle and the speed a steamer's smoke is blown by it, the speed of the clouds racing overhead, and the conditions of the sea, though whenever you are racing in the shallow waters of the North Sea, where the tides are fairly strong, you always think there is more wind than there really is. The same applies when standing on a lee shore; you hear the seas breaking in on the beach, and as sound has much to do with our judgment, you think there is more wind than is really the case. Actually the wind on a lee shore is often like a big blustering bully, merely noisy and with little guts in it.

146

This is only general, and to try and help you form your ideas of the speed of the wind; once you get sailing you soon see if you are over-canvassed.

As you know, I have raced and sailed in every type of boat and in a great many countries, over a fair number of years, and am trying to condense the knowledge I have gained into this series of letters. To bring points out more clearly I shall always tend to exaggerate, as by so doing I make a definite statement and this will conjure up a more definite picture in your mind. For instance, you must remember that a lee shore is a dangerous shore, as you have only to make one mistake to feel the full weight of the wind, which, as I have said, was like a 'blustering bully' with little guts in it, and when you feel this weight you will realise that there are some guts and power in it, as the chances are you will be driven ashore and wrecked.

I hope this letter will give you a good idea of the winds, which at all times you must study very intently, as they are the only power you have to sail with, and the thing to do is to use them sensibly and not stupidly, for like fire they are a good friend but a bad master.

P.S. With this letter on the wind, a postscript of tides and currents caused by them seems most fitting. The tides, as you know, are governed by the moon, and during the full moon or a new moon they are at their highest and called spring tides. The latter occur every two weeks, and between these times the tides are very dead and are called neap tides. At Cowes, for instance, the springs rise and fall 14 ft, and the neaps only 8ft, and this rise and fall, as can easily be imagined, causes tidal streams or currents. It is easy to understand that during the spring tides the currents are much stronger than during neaps, and more allowance must be made for the tidal streams during spring tides. Tidal streams, generally speaking, run parallel with the shore, the flood running some six hours one way, and the ebb six hours in the opposite direction.

The tides must be studied carefully, for the streams caused by them either help or hinder you and by how much can easily be calculated in this way. Supposing you are sailing four miles an hour against a three-mile stream, you are only going over the ground one mile an hour, but if you have the three-mile-an-hour stream with you, you are travelling seven miles an hour, the difference being double the speed of the tide. Also, when the tide is high, it is often possible to sail over rocks and banks which at low tide are standing out of the water.

The wind affects the tide strongly; for instance, here at Cowes in the English channel, the flood tide runs from west to east, and so it is easy to imagine this stream increasing in speed with a hard westerly wind, and as well as an increase in the speed of the flood stream, the tide is higher than normal, and an easterly wind blowing against the flood tide makes for a smaller tide and slower tidal stream.

In places where the tidal stream is very strong, and there are points of rocks or land sticking out unfairly into it, you will find an eddy running in the opposite direction almost as fast as the main stream itself, an important point often overlooked by racing people, so watch for this whenever you are racing in tidal waters.

Another point to watch for is the turn of the tide. In every part of the world that I have visited the tide has always turned earlier inshore by some one or more hours, and by working this, it is possible to pick up a fair tide much earlier than your opponents, the rule being to carry on offshore during the last of the fair tide, and then to go right in under the land, as by doing this you will have carried the last drains of one tide, and then by going close into the land you will pick up the earliest part of the new tide, and with the tide changing every six hours, it is possible to have nine hours of fair tide and only three hours of foul tide, because you are actually working tides that change one and a half hours earlier and later than each other. To study the tides is one of the first things you should do when arriving to race in strange waters, for you will never win a race by following other people, and with a little intelligence you will soon find out enough of the tidal streams to enable you to win races in strange waters. The shape of the land, the bays and points all tell you just what to expect the tide to do.

Yours UFFA."

That letter, read today, is as fresh as when Uffa wrote it in 1936. That it went unnoticed by many of those who began to sail dinghies in the late Forties and Fifties, is almost incredulous. Its sound advice should be taken by anyone starting to sail. Uffa also knew that a well prepared boat was important in winning races.

Canoe *Brynhild*,
Perios Guirrec

My dear Michael,
The last letter was about the power that drives your little boat, and this one is about the boat herself and her care and maintenance.

In the first instance you must bear in mind that to you she is rather like a violin to a musician, she has to be cared for and tuned, so that she is right up to concert pitch for every race, and this means a lot of knowledge and preparation. Her outside must be well looked after and perfectly smooth, her mast and rigging must be as near perfection as is possible, while her sails should be in keeping with the rest; and this letter is to try and tell you how to do these things.

First of all the outside. She already has some twelve or more coats of varnish on her, but though this sounds a lot there is no thickness in it, as every coat has been rubbed down before the next has been applied and whenever she needs varnishing you should rub her down most carefully with a wet glasspaper, generally known as 'wet' or 'dry', the reason for using it wet being that when wet the glasspaper grinds the surface down, whereas if dry it scratches rather than grinds. After rubbing her down wash her off well with some fresh water, and let her dry thoroughly. Then apply the varnish (with a brush) as thick as you can without it running, for an even coat of varnish flowed on with the brush will not show any brush marks, but will settle down into a mirror-like surface.

Nowadays the rigging does most of the supporting of the mast, the mast itself being little more than a strut under compression, all the side loads being taken by the wires extended over the struts or crosstrees, and so you see that everything depends on the tension

149

on the wires. If they are slack the mast will bend so far before the wires start to do their work, so it is very important to have every wire with the correct tension on it, and different masts and different sized boats need different tensions on their wires. On your boat *Whisper* you should have (this is only a rough guide) about 150 lbs on the shrouds and forestay when at rest and 90 lbs on your diamond shrouds, but as I said before different masts need different tensions, so study your own mast and see just what tension is best for it.

Many owners worry too much about these tensions, and others not enough, and I would say over this point find out what is best for your mast, which you can do in a very short while, and then keep to it, not altering anything at all unless absolutely necessary, as then you will always go out in exactly the same trim without your mast causing you a moment's anxiety, so leaving all your energies and thoughts free for racing.

The Sails. These when new should be stretched in the lightest of airs with sunshine. Then you will find them stretch evenly all over, but because they are so small, some six hours of sailing will stretch a dinghy mainsail and a jib. A shower of rain does not seem to hurt them, neither does the wet as long as they are dried afterwards, and by the look of the sails on *Brynhild*, which have had a pretty rough time this last 300 miles, it would almost seem that like wives, the harder they are treated the better they are, but this I cannot think is true, for no general rule is ever true of all, so it would seem that the better you can care for your sails the better they will set.

Yours UFFA**"**

From 'Sail and Power' *by Uffa Fox*

Those who ever sailed dinghies with cotton sails will remember the importance of the last part of that letter, the advent of man-made fibres has made life a good deal easier but they still benefit from proper care. Watching the better sailors looking after their boats and sails is an object lesson.

In Uffa's day, the Fourteen was one of the few dinghies raced on a national basis; it was the first class to be accorded international status by the International Yacht Racing Union. It held then, as it does on a more widespread basis now, a camaraderie among the protagonists at its regattas. It is the veritable King of dinghies and, as a development class, continues to impress new followers all over the world. One Fourteen design was used on the first ever professional circus because the class offered such sensational racing to the competitors and spectators alike. Uffa would have liked that.

So too would Bruce Banks – The Druid – whose *Windsprite* had a long run of successes. Her conception and birth are part of a chapter in a book by Keith Shackleton, the naturalist and artist who crewed her many times.

"*Windsprite* was built at Wolverstone shipyard near Ipswich to the combined drawings and ideas of Bruce Banks and Austin Farrar, who for some inexplicable reason is always called Clarence. Like all small boat design it was the embodiment of several compromises, yet there were some audacious extremes in her lines which trial alone could test and prove. Her hull was shaped on a prepared mould and carefully glued, her outer skin laid fore and aft, her inner diagonal, so she was smooth and ribless inside, and bore a look of functional simplicity not unlike that of a well-appointed bath. Her name was chosen by Bruce to follow a long line of compound words embodying 'wind' for the names of all his previous boats. I remember that he stuck steadfastly to this particular choice in spite of a number of suggested alternatives. It was not that any of us disliked the name, but more that we believed we could think of a better one.

It is interesting to trace the design and development of the International Fourteens, because they are a restricted but not a one-design boat. Within a tolerant set of rules their shape can be altered to allow for experiment, provided they are bound by an overall length and minimum beam and weight. Minor rules to these provide that they shall always be an open boat to preserve the art of sailing them dry in a seaway, which is surely one of the great challenges of seamanship. This may seem like an old-fashioned

151

belief, but insomuch as we sail for satisfaction and enjoyment, it is an important one, and I believe should be kept that way. The fact that trout are more easily caught on a worm would not be justification enough to lure one away from the absorbing delight of working a fly.

It has generally been found that a development in one direction or another, though providing a faster boat at one point of sailing, would make her slower on another, and so the attempt has always gone on in the hope of finding a hull with the greatest number of advantages and the fewest drawbacks. By 1946, after over twenty years of designing – principally by Morgan Giles and Uffa Fox – a hull shape had been reached for the class which seemed to give the best all-round performance, and for a little while following it there was no marked change. Then all at once in 1948 a new conception was reached and boats were built in large numbers by Fairey Marine at Hamble to the new set of lines by Uffa Fox. It was a boat with a wider beam and a flatter run aft, and proved faster off the wind than anything yet produced. In the following year it won for England a series of international races in Canada and gained terrific success at the hands of Charles Currey in Bermuda. But fast though it was in heavy weather off the wind, it could be beaten to windward by the narrower boats which had finer bows and a way of cutting the water with a minimum of fuss rather than slamming through the rough with a full wide bow, slowing themselves against the continual thump of the waves.

So *Windsprite* came into being as another compromise between the two. She had fine bows and an even flatter run, and more width at the transom to give her power. When she was lifted off the mould and stood on the quay, bare and unfitted, she somehow looked right. There is no need to be a naval architect to recognise this quality, because it comes more from intuition than from specialised knowledge. There are certain types of aeroplanes which appear to have an inherent desire to fly, as if conscious that the air is their real medium and their ground time an irksome wait between flights. There are others which obviously would fly, and will, if enough power be provided but their whole demeanour suggest a certain reluctance. It is the first category which invariably succeeds.

Windsprite was like this. She looked fast off the wind, and better still she looked as if she would go well to windward, and as if the whole rough and smooth of sailing performance was going to succeed in her. What was more, though I scarcely dared mention or even think it at the time, she looked capable of winning the Prince of Wales Cup.

Now came the human element. *Whisper*, the old Fourteen who will later be more fully described, had gone to the West Country, and for a short while following this I had no boat of my own, and sailing days were spent in learning something about crewing and fishing for mackerel. The advent of *Windsprite* and the new enterprise came as one of those very happy decisions both timely and fortunate which come without warning and make for a turning-point or a milestone in one's life. I remember being brought into it on Boxing Day 1949, when for some far-fetched reason Bruce and I were sailing a twelve-foot National down the harbour from Itchenor. There was ice everywhere and we could scarcely move under the boom for duffel coats, nor get our toes under the straps for the sea-boots we wore. It was an unusual situation and was supposed to have something to do with getting Christmas out of the system, though I never really conceded that as an advantage. It was a memorable day, however; we saw a peregrine take a widgeon off Cobnor Point, and we had some rum aboard. Before we got back the plan was made, and I found myself drawn into the most exciting and instructive days of racing I shall ever know.

We fitted *Windsprite* out together, putting into her all the odds and ends we each preferred. Her most impressive piece of equipment was the reefing gear to be buried in the mast, and which was made up of the most intricate collection of well-oiled and shining mechanical items, the function of which were wholly beyond my understanding. I knew it simply as the only device yet discovered that really took the irk out of reefing, both rolling the boom and slackening off the halyard in one. Since then it has

153

proved itself a success and many have been made and gone into small boats, adding much to their seaworthiness and the comfort of their sailing without bending any purist principles. As we drove up to Ipswich at the time, I had the parts of it in a biscuit tin on my knee and tried to fit one into the other with Bruce's occasional instruction from the driving seat. It was quite incomprehensible to me that any human could make such a thing in his own home, even if he were able to hit upon the idea of it in the first place. By the time we reached Colchester, Bruce had taken the tin and contents from me and put it in the back with the air of one taking articles from a child when there is a danger of his swallowing them. 'There is no need to understand the theory of it', he said, 'so long as you can work it'. And that seemed reasonable enough to me, for by all accounts a chimpanzee could shorten sail with this device while laughing over his shoulder and sucking an orange. As events worked out it was a pity there were so few chances to use it in practice.

We worked long and late on *Windsprite* in the yard, bit by bit getting her ready for the sea, fortifying ourselves with tea, biscuits, and anecdotes into the small hours, and finally creeping into Ipswich for fish and chips last thing. A Yacht Racing Association measurer with a big heart helped us finish her, measured her for her class certificate, and passed her buoyancy test in the Orwell. She was complete.

It was a whole week before we could do more, and the days passed slowly in the anticipation of her first sail. Bruce chose Poole Harbour for the event, because it was both near his home and far from witnesses. Here she could be tried out in secret, and if the worst happened we would be spared rude laughter. Self-consciously we looked both ways and slipped her in. The first test was over: 'She floats', he said.

From the start it seemed that she would be a sympathetic boat; she reefed and unreefed smoothly and surely, the plate came up and down on the new hoist in beautiful style – only once or twice giving an anxious moment when a stone found its way into the works as they say spanners will, and locked it fully down. The halyard winches ran with the ease of fishing reels, and all that day Bruce wore a special grin which is kept for moments of great success; I was to see that on several more occasions with this boat.

In her first few races she did quite well as she shook herself down. Once her rudder broke in a squall and we capsized; the plate hoist jammed a few more times and we had to swim under her and fix it for fear of breaking the plate. And so the teething troubles went through in the fashion of every other boat. At the same time we got to know each other, and that made it possible to wring a little more out of her here and there when it really mattered. At last she was ready. There was nothing more that could be done to better her. She was towed up to Hunstanton for the Prince of Wales Cup late at night, each driving some of the way, with the mind – nearly the car at times – distracted from the road by an unusually spectacular show of the Northern Lights.

Written accounts of races are duller to read than the events themselves are to watch, but we had a wonderful week there. She won three of the five races, including the Prince of Wales Cup itself. I could never forget the sensation of the first gun over the broken water as she crossed the line in flying sheets of spray with a straight white wake behind her; we were soaked to the skin and exultantly happy; I could not believe in a greater feeling of content at that moment, but it must have been a small thing beside that of Bruce – not only for sailing her but for hatching her with Clarence out of much thought and sheets of paper.

In the painting she is reaching with spinnaker set as it was on the second last leg of the course. The sky and sea were ragged from the wind, and in the deeper water of the Wash a swell ran long and slowly, so that she would swing up to the top and plane down the face of each successive sea. I shall remember her this way not just because of her success but because these conditions seemed to be of her own choice, she responded to them with a hum in the wires and a real skip in her tread. There is a scraperboard drawing of her standing on the stage, and on her foredeck is a half-pint mug to illustrate the camber of her bow tank, and for the fun of putting in a little reflection underneath. People always stand glasses here

155

when they stop to gossip and there are many interlocked rings and semicircles like the symbol of the Olympic Games, some of them made by liquors corrosive enough to be nearly through to the wood. She is well baptised now and has won again twice with Bruce in the Prince of Wales Cup – once in a sunny calm in Plymouth Sound and once in a wild turmoil of wind and sea off Lowestoft. She is a very good boat.**"**

From 'Wake' by Keith Shackleton

'Fourteens are Forever', says the advertising slogan of the class. Their heritage and pedigree are superb and those who administer the class appear to have put it on the right lines but how would those who banned the trapeze, after Peter Scott and John Winter had won the Prince of Wales Cup using one, think about the current twin trapeze Fourteen? They would count for little anyway. A better slogan for the class might be 'Forever is Today'.

Chapter Nine

The Story-tellers Tales

Yachting, as a sport, has always been well chronicled as indeed have the off-the-water activities of many of its major players. What has generally escaped the public notice, and often for very good reasons, are the sometimes racy goings-on of the chroniclers themselves. I refer not only to the activist meetings of our own organisation, the Society of International Nautical Scribes (SINS) with its own peer group of International Commodores, but to the ways in which some have chased their stories.

In those halcyon days of big yacht racing between the wars, the contemporary yachting writers led a far more refined life than their counterparts of today. It is a far cry from the days of Brooke Heckstall-Smith, universally known as 'Bookstall', standing close to King George V on the afterdeck of *Britannia* to scrabbling on the dockside post-race trying to interview the winning skipper. 'Bookstall' wasn't alone although that great East Coast photographer Douglas Went, who was privileged to take my portrait at six and a half weeks, used to row out to the big boats when they raced at Harwich and Southend to capture but a single shot per race and compares well with today's motor-driven, multi-bodied, long-lens paparazzi who force themselves and their equipment into small inflatables so that they can record the action on film; uncomfortable but in the right place most of the time.

We do, despite the increased public awareness of yachting – and sometimes because of it – have, from time to time, to try to snatch a story that for reasons is denied to us. How much we would have given, say, for the scuba equipment and the knowledge of its use that two members of a rival syndicate's crew had on the first night that *Australia II* was hoisted in her slings with her security skirt around her winged keel, back in 1983. That story would have been worth a thing or two but it could well have changed the path of the *America*'s Cup.

My old friend Jack Knights split a pair of trousers during a nocturnal expedition close to the Franco-Swiss border, coming out of the window of a building shed in Eggar's yard as the hull of Baron Bich's experimental 12-Metre, *Chanceggar*, neared completion. That, however, was only a quarter of a century ago; one hundred years before that, in December 1866, Stephen Fiske was given an assignment that he was determined to carry through despite the well-intentioned actions of some friends to prevent him. Stephen Fiske must go down as the all-time embodiment of a newshound.

Fiske was a reporter for the *New York Herald*, a newspaper owned by James Gordon Bennett Sr, and his assignment came from the top. It was to cover the first ever ocean race, from Sandy Hook to the Needles, aboard the 205-ton schooner *Henrietta*, the property of James Gordon Bennett Jr., son of the proprietor. Anyone can see the necessity of Fiske to travel as planned but there were among his friends those who considered the voyage a foolhardy one, one which put Fiske's life at risk.

In order to protect their friend, they arranged for him to be subpoenaed to appear as a witness in a court case and a couple of tipstaffs were sent to the gangway of the steamer *P.C.Schultz*, the boat which Fiske was to board to take him to the *Henrietta* early on the morning of 11 December 1886. Happily, Fiske saw the tipstaffs before they spotted him and quickly edged down the Desbrosses Street Pier (now lost in the in-filling on the lower west side of Manhattan) away from the steamer. He was not to be deterred however, and bribed his way aboard the New York Yacht Club's members spectator steamer, *River Queen*, by the simple expedient of giving a stevedore some money to allow him to carry on a case of champagne.

'Once aboard the lugger . . .', goes the cry, but for Fiske the task of dodging the tipstaffs and making it aboard the *Henrietta* was still a tricky one. It was one which, nevertheless, provided Fiske with an opportunity to display his schoolboy sense of humour.

The *River Queen* had considerable historic importance. She had been owned by President Abraham Lincoln and down below, the assassinated President's cabin had been roped off, a show-case tribute to the man. As the members of the NYYC and their guests tripped down, often tipsily, to see the shrine, they would have thought that the figure hunched at Lincoln's desk was a waxwork. Far from it, it was none other than the living Stephen Fiske.

That day, there was considerable detective activity afoot on the waters of New York Harbour. A supposed Fenian plot to use the race as a means of smuggling the leader of the Irish Republican Brotherhood in America, James Stephens, to England had been alerted by the British Home Secretary. The police proved to be none to bright and were seemingly chasing rainbows. Their best idea was that Stephens was the sailing master of the *Henrietta* and that all three schooners in the race were Fenian privateers. With all this going on however, Fiske decided that he would leave his moves to the very last moment.

A tall man, who admitted that he had 'a sizeable problem' with his escape plan, he wrote of his activities in the *Herald*:

❝I waited in my waxwork semblance till all the presidential spectators flew up on deck when the yachts at their anchorage at Stapleton came in sight. Then I went up behind and mingled with them, having removed my beard and side-whiskers in the late president's toilet room.

The *River Queen* came so closely alongside the *P.C.Schultz* at one point that I had no difficulty in grasping the hand of a supposed friend aboard the *Schultz* – a man who was considerably more than three sheets in the wind and who was as ready to welcome me as if I had truly been a long-lost companion of his youth. Pretending the same state myself I clambered over the rail of the *River Queen* and made a hazardous leap to the deck of the other vessel. Staggering about a little, I managed to convey to many cheering witnesses that my athletic feat had been of the charmed kind always achieved by the drunken and I made no more than a fleeting impression – there was so much cheering, gallivanting, and dancing going on, and the tension was so high, that the odd appeared perfectly ordinary.

From then on my method was clear. The cargo of wines and provisions was piled in the hold of the *Schultz* with the hatches off and it was in no way difficult to persuade one of the crew detailed for the loading to accept a five-dollar contribution to his welfare and prise open one of the cases and secrete me therein in lieu of the champagne. I had the greatest of cricks and cramps as a result, but my object was achieved. I was swung aboard the *Henrietta* and pushed up the lid of my temporary abode to come face-to-face with my master-cum-employer for the duration of this trifling journey across the Atlantic."

New York Herald

One can imagine how James Gordon Bennett Jr. must have felt at this jack-in-the-box appearance of Fiske, unless he had been following in the footsteps of his friends and celebrating his departure in style. Fiske was on board and began his reporting immediately. He was a man who knew a story when he saw one and was determined to make the most of it. He recorded for posterity one of the great sea yarns of all time.

To some determination is sometimes not enough, even for the best of yachting reporters and there is no doubt that Australia's Bob Ross is one of those. In 1973, Alan Bond's first 12-Metre had been trucked across the country from her builders, Halvorsen, Morson & Gowland in Sydney, to her base at Yanchep Sun City (known to its detractors as 'Ratshit Fly City') a few miles north of Perth. She was hauled out of the water in a shed – the precursor of Bond's security screening of *Australia II*'s keel. The world wanted to see the underbody of this Bob Miller (later Ben Lexcen) design, not the least of them Bob Ross.

The end doors of the shed opened on to the little harbour at Yanchep and right opposite them was a cray fishing boat at her mooring. Bob did a deal with the owner that he could stay on board for a couple of days so that he could see what was in there when the doors were opened. Two days and nights passed and the cray fisherman wanted to go about his business once again. The doors hadn't opened and Bob returned home to Sydney a touch disappointed.

Sometimes, luck runs one's way. A few weeks later, I was passing through Perth and made a pilgrimage to Yanchep early one morning – I had heard of the size and viciousness of the flies in the heat of the day! It must have been around breakfastime when I arrived and made my way to the seven-foot-high chain link fence around the shed. The gate was open. I walked in and tried the shed door, having never been against some minor trespassing. It opened and in I went to see the white bottom of the yellow hull of *Southern Cross*.

There was, I promise, no one about. I took out my camera with a wide angle lens and shot off a few frames. I had just finished that and was gazing upwards at the stern when into the shed came Rob Sterling, the 'Wharf Rat', a member of the crew.

'G'day Bob', then, with realisation, 'What the hell are you doing in here. You'll get me fired. I'm on security'. The 'Rat' was rattled. I was quickly escorted from the giant hanger and Rob and I went over to the crew quarters for a cup of coffee. As we walked Rob pointed to my camera. 'Did you take any photos', he asked. 'Would I do a thing like that', I countered rhetorically. The reply seemed to satisfy him but he added, 'I'd feel happier if you put it away'.

Three days later I flew to Sydney and walked into the office where Bob Ross sat working under considerable pressure. In my hand was a roll of Kodak Tri-X and I said, 'Can you get this processed for me'. 'Sure', said Bob, tossing it idly into a tray on his desk. He hadn't any idea what was on that film so I thought he ought to know. 'Bob', I said, 'there are a few frames there which might interest you, of the underwater body of *Southern Cross* in her shed, the ones I believe you spent two days trying to capture'. Bob reached for the film as he rose and disappeared rapidly out of the door muttering, 'I'll be back'. The material, not who had obtained it or how, was the important factor.

Just as the syndicates, in the Newport summer of 1974, seemed obsessed by having secrets, there were those among us who were equally as

161

determined to pry into them. For us barbed wire held no terrors; it may have ripped Jack Knights' trousers but he obtained a scoop in return. That I remembered as I recalled in my book, *12-Metre Images*, in another escapade in search of a story, Jack very much in mind.

"I thought of him six years later in Newport when I went in search of information, also in the middle of the night and also faced with a barbed-wire fence. I had got wind of a magical device that was being used aboard *Courageous*, about which none of her crew was prepared to talk but about which plenty of rumour was circulating. It was suggested that she had an on-board computer which provided her afterguard with rapid information about the true wind speed and direction, and navigational data that no one had ever had before.

Courageous came out of the water – overnight resting in hoists was not a regular feature of 1974 – for some work to be carried out on her bottom about a month before the cup, when she was still involved in selection trials with *Intrepid*. I noticed her in the yard near the Goat Island bridge, and the temptation became overwhelming. I excused myself early from David Ray's famous Newport watering hole, the Candy Store, went to bed and set my alarm for 0330.

Dressed in dark slacks and a black sweater, I drove down to the yard and parked close to the fence so that the car would provide me with a start to climbing over it. I took with me a camera with flash-gun, torch and notebook. Straddling the fence, I remembered Knights and took great care. Once in the yard I found a short ladder and climbed into *Courageous*, under the tarpaulin with which she was covered to keep the rain out. Down below I headed for the navigation station to meet Sidney Greybox.

Named after his casing, Sidney was a much modified Data General Nova 1200 mini-computer which the *Courageous* syndicate had installed as an alternative to running a trial horse throughout the summer. The syndicate felt that the alternative was cheaper and more accurate. To modify the computer and to make it effective for their purposes, they appointed Rich McCurdy of the Kenyon Instrument Company as consultant, and it was he who considered Sidney his baby.

I pointed the torch at the schedule taped to the side of the boat which listed Sidney's various functions and wrote them down in my notebook. I set my camera and twice photographed the entire set-up; it seemed like three years while the flash-gun recharged. Then it was out of the boat and back over the fence, taking great care not to catch anything on the barbed wire, and away to my bed.

Some four hours later I headed for a breakfast bar, only to sit alongside Rich McCurdy at the counter. We exchanged pleasantries and the conversation drifted, inevitably, around to the computer on *Courageous*. Rich did not seem to mind that I made notes as we went along, and as we finished our meal he said, 'Do you want to come over to see it? Bring your camera with you'. I have never dared to tell him what I was doing a few hours before!"

From '12-Metre Images' by Bob Fisher

It's an interesting life we lead, packed full of action but always time for the odd jest. Bob Ross, with whom I have spent many happy hours came out tops on this exchange.

We were relaxing in a 25-foot fast motorboat on Lake Ontario at the pre-Olympic regatta in 1975. The sun beat down from a cloudless sky and we were at the gybe mark on the Tempest and Soling course; we had gone there after the second start and had had a little time in hand. Our hosts offered us a couple of cold tins of the refreshing fluid and after we had had a good pull each, I looked at Bob and said, more directed at our two companions, 'You know, the life of a yachting writer isn't all beer and skittles'. 'No', said Bob languidly, 'I haven't had a game for weeks!'

The games people play is what amuses us and provides us with our stories. Sometimes we find ourselves at the forefront of the story and the odd first person singular report is added to our cuttings file. Like the occasion in 1983 when Dick Pratt, the syndicate head of the Melbourne entered *Challenge 12*, decided to put some fun back into the *America*'s

Cup. To do so, he took a Newport mansion for the evening and gave a sizeable dinner party. Some members of the media were invited, because Dick had planned the odd joke or two. Trouble was, the evening backfired horribly.

Dick's first mistake was that he invited former Australian Prime Minister Malcolm Fraser to speak. Fraser, fresh from a conference with similarly deposed prime ministers from around the world at Vail, was up to speed in the speaking stakes and used this opportunity to align the heritage of Australia and America on the grounds that they had both been founded by 'English undesirables', and then he went on to add that the most undesirables were still left in England. Of course, there was a titter or two, but most of them were from released embarrassment than from amusement as the Marchioness of Milford Haven was present at the dinner. Worse was to come when Fraser went on to say later that if anyone thought that he should apologise, he certainly was not going to.

What came next took the evening from bad to worse. Aussie comedian, Campbell McComas, in a badly briefed satirical review, hit hard at those who had been involved in the Cup's history. After a particularly snide remark at Bus Mosbacher, a former Cup winner, his wife stood up with the retort, 'I've had enough'. So saying, she swept out accompanied by her husband. It was an ugly moment.

After the sort of dreaded silence that no one likes to break, we were back at trying to help Dick put the fun back into the *America*'s Cup. He was providing the fun juice and we decided that some of it should be consumed. Time came, however, when I felt it was time to retrieve my moped – valet-parked, naturally – and I stopped to say farewell and thank you to my host, adding that I had enjoyed myself, 'even though I am a Pom!'

Fraser, standing alongside Dick, simply gloated, 'I wonder you didn't leave'. There are times when a shut mouth is best, but not after that; I could not resist the counter: 'No sweat. I've been insulted by experts. I don't take any notice of has-beens!'

My father, I am sure, would have had a giggle at that. It was he who told me, very early in my working life, that I had a decision to make. 'You can either be rich', he said, 'or a yachting writer'. I always maintain that I took the hard way in life. There are of course others who believe that the life of a journalist affords, like the French widow in Gerard Hoffnung's *Letters from Tyrolean Landlords*, 'delightful prospects', one of them being that great seafarer Alan Villiers.

"While I was in a quandary as to what to do, my friend from the *Aristides* and I chanced to be waiting outside the Hobart town-hall one Sunday afternoon, waiting for the doors to open for a musical concert, when a small car drove up to the newspaper office opposite, and a smart young man got out. He was well dressed and appeared prosperous. My shipmate knew him, and they exchanged greetings. The smart young man let himself into a side-door of the newspaper building, and I wondered what he could be doing there.

'Why, that's Jack Williams, from Devonport,' my friend told me. 'He's a newspaper reporter – you know, a journalist. He works for the *Mercury* here. I expect he's gone in there to write up his report of something or other from last night, in time for tomorrow's paper'.

A newspaper reporter? Why, this was just the thing for me! Until then I had never thought of journalism as a profession I could enter. The Labour journals for which my father wrote paid nothing, and dealt only in propaganda. I had not realised that young men were employed to report news. From the appearance of Mr Williams the profession must be a profitable one. The possession of an automobile was itself a mark of affluence. No sailor, I knew, could afford such a thing in Australia. It came to me almost with the suddenness of a bomb-burst that newspaper reporting was just the thing that I could do.

It was all very well to decide that I intended to become a journalist, but how could I set about it? The only possible approach, I thought, was the direct one. I had no influence and no Tasmanian friends. The thing to do, I thought, was to prepare a note requesting an interview, and take the note along to the newspaper office myself. So upon the Monday morning I took an hour's leave from the jam factory and presented myself at the front office of the *Mercury*, with a request to see the editor. I did not know that editors of morning newspapers were rarely in their offices in the morning. My note was sent to the manager, who must have been a kindly man. At any rate, a message that a sailor was outside who wished

165

to become a journalist was sufficient to open his door. It was my great good fortune that I had hit upon one of those men who would themselves have loved to lead just the life I had been leading, to whom the great sailing-ship was almost as compellingly attractive as it was to me. Tasmania abounded in ship-loving citizens, for its maritime history was recent, great, and stirring. I don't doubt that the *Mercury's* manager would have gone off in a Cape Horner, if he could. He received me pleasantly, and I was soon at my ease.

'I should like', I said, 'to become a newspaper reporter'. What were my qualifications? Well, I had done fairly well at school and had matriculated, with a scholarship: I had served several years in deep-sea sailing-ships, and had wandered over some part of the world; I thought I could at least make a job of a column in the *Mercury* headed 'Shipping Intelligence', which was neither very accurate about ships nor particularly intelligent; I liked writing concise accounts of things. Well, he said, not very gratified by my remark about his shipping column, the young junior who writes that covers the Hobart magistrate's court, fire-stations, and hospitals as well, and does a turn of telephone duty in the evenings, taking down in shorthand news 'phoned in by district correspondents'. How should I get on with all that? His reporter's knowledge of shipping might be deficient in some points, but he had served four years as a cadet and junior reporter, and had been a copy-holder in the readers' room for a year before that. He could write shorthand and use a typewriter. He knew the *Mercury* style, and its sources of information.

The manager went on to point out that in order to become a reporter at all, it was necessary to serve a three-years' cadetship; and to be selected as a cadet one must first serve at least twelve months in the readers' room to learn something of the ropes. There were already four youths in that room waiting for the chance to become cadet reporters and some had been waiting two years. There was also a list of young gentlemen, well recommended by their schools, who were waiting to enter the reading room.

The manager said I could come back that evening to discuss the matter with the head reader, if I wished, and if I would send in the journals I had kept aboard my various ships, he would read them with interest. I should have to learn to write shorthand at least 120 words a minute, and be prepared to reach licensed shorthand writers' standard, for the *Mercury* took its verbatim reports seriously and provided the State Parliament with its records. I should also be required to learn how to use a typewriter, at my own expense. If I was prepared to do all these things, and to spend a least a year in the proof-reading room, my name might be added to the waiting list.

When I called on the head reader that evening I learned that the prospects were even slimmer than the manager had suggested. A copy-holder, I gathered, was a youth who read aloud from the reporters' manuscript or typescript while a proof-reader corrected the proofs, in order to ensure that what was printed was, at any rate, what had been written down. To begin with, I should earn no more than 25s. or 30s. a week, and my board in Campbell Street cost more than that. There were far more applicants than there were vacancies. The *Mercury* was a comfortable office and, once employed there, people rarely left. Sometimes the more enterprising spirits did migrate to Melbourne or Sydney, where he said, there was a steady demand for *Mercury*-trained journalists. I gathered that, to stand a chance of reaching even the first low rung of the ladder to a real newspaper job, I should have to wait either until a member of the editorial or reading staff died, or some young man decided to try his fortune in one of the mainland capitals.

The head reader took down my name and temporary address, and advised me to keep the job I had until a vacancy occurred at the *Mercury*. But I could keep my job only as long as the fruit season lasted, and that was ending. Weeks passed. I heard nothing from the newspaper office. A month passed. I wrote. The head reader acknowledged the letter. No vacancies yet, he said. Two months passed. I was without a job. At dawn I was outside the *Mercury* office reading the front page which was posted there to see if there were any jobs I could go after, and I began to wonder whether that was as close as I would ever get to that or any other newspaper office. I hawked insurance for a very short spell. That was no job for me. Meanwhile

I had enroled myself at a local business college, learning shorthand and typewriting at night with a group of merry Tasmanian girls whose studies were not always confined to the curriculum of the business school. I read avidly and studied anything I could get hold of which had any bearing on the newspaper life."

From 'The Set of the Sails' by Alan Villiers

The good news is that he was eventually taken on by the Hobart *Mercury*, as I am given to believe was Errol Flynn for a time, which is why, perhaps, his books about the sailing ships are always so well written. The other good news is that he had many more ocean passages to make in sailing ships, thereby leaving the door open for another journalist to fill his shoes at the *Mercury* and the world to enjoy the tales he had to tell.

Jack Knights, while he lived and sailed, was a fund of tales. Once he was testing a singlehanded dinghy with a sliding seat off Cowes and was coming into the mouth of the Medina, just off the Royal Yacht Squadron Castle when he was hailed by one of those plummy voices that are found in the 'Gin & Tonic' Brigade.

'I say, number three', for that was the number of Jack's sail, 'what class are you?'

'Lower middle', replied Jack unabashed.

On another occasion when we were sailing together in his quarter-tonner, *Odd Job*, I had begun to steer downwind in a fresh breeze at night after rounding the Needles Fairway buoy. Jack had steered the beat all the way from Weymouth and as we were bound for the CH1 buoy off Cherbourg, Jack had decided to get his head down for a while and had gone below. Suddenly in answer to a hefty pull on the tiller to correct the wilful behaviour of this boat, the whole unit came off the rudder head. *Odd Job* rounded up sharpish and Jack's head popped up in the companionway.

'Can't you keep this thing going the right way?'

I couldn't resist it. 'Here, you try' I said, handing him tiller and extension.

Far from winning, I was left with no doubt as to what we could do. Jack passed a big wrench from the tool-box and suggested that I put that on the squared off top of the rudder post and used it as a tiller.

Bibliography

Wake by Keith Shackleton. Published by William Clowes and Sons Ltd, London 1954.

Sailing Tours by Frank Cowper, Vol 1. Published by L. Upcott Gill, London 1892.

Blue Water, Green Skipper by Stuart Woods. Published by Stanford Maritime Ltd, London 1977. (Now A&C Black Ltd)

Moxie by Phil Weld. Published by Little, Brown & Co, USA 1972 and 1981.

Sacred Cowes, by Anthony Heckstall-Smith. Published by Anthony Blond Ltd, London 1965 (second edition).

Sail and Power by Uffa Fox. Peter Davies Ltd, London 1936.

Amateur Sailing by Tyrrel E.Biddle. Published by Norie & Wilson, London 1886.

Tom Diaper's Log. Published by Robert Ross & Co Ltd 1950.

Voyage of the Cap Pilar by Adrian Seligman. Published by Hodder and Stoughton Ltd, London 1939.

Come Hell or High Water by Clare Francis. Published by Pelham Books, London 1977.

Jottings for the Young Sailor by L.F. Cunningham. Published by Captain O.M. Watts, London 1938.

The Art of Course Sailing by Michael Green. Published by Hutchinson & Co Ltd., London, May 1962.

12-Metre Images by Bob Fisher. Published by Pelham Books 1986.

Last of the Wind Ships by Alan Villiers. Published by George Routledge and Sons, London, 1935.

Project Cheers by Tom Follett, Dick Newick, Jim Morris. Published by Adlard Coles Ltd, London 1969. (Now A&C Black Ltd)

The Set of the Sails by Alan Villiers. Published by Hodder and Stoughton, London 1949.

Sailorman by E.G. Martin OBE. Published by Oxford University Press, London.

Sailing Alone Around the World by Joshua Slocum. Published by Sampson Low, Marston & Co Ltd, circa 1930.

Catamaran Racing by Reg White and Bob Fisher. Published by Cassell, London 1968.

Enterprise by Harold S. Vanderbilt. Published by Charles Scribner's Sons New York 1931.

The Twelve-Meter Challenges for the America's Cup by Norris D. Hoyt. Published by E.P. Dutton, New York.

The Grand Gesture by Roger Vaughan. Published by Little Brown & Co, Boston.

Death at Newport by Derryn Hinch. Published by Angus & Robertson, Australia.

Racing for the America's Cup – The view from the Candy Store by Theodore A. Jones. Published by New York Times Book Co.

Blake's Odyssey by Peter Blake and Alan Sefton. Published by Hodder and Stoughton, Auckland 1982.